徐文虎　许闲　主编

复旦保险教育百年纪念画册

复旦大学出版社

复旦保险教育百年纪念画册编委会

顾问

施岳群　张　军　陈诗一　张　怡

名誉主编

洪远朋

主编

徐文虎　许　闲

编委会

尚汉冀	复旦大学友邦－复旦精算中心
赵兰亮	复旦大学历史学系
张红明	复旦大学校史馆
尹　晔	复旦大学发展研究院中国保险与社会安全研究中心
张　兴	复旦大学保险校友会
吴海晓	复旦大学保险校友会
王广智	复旦大学保险校友会
丁　纯	复旦大学经济学院世界经济系
李荣敏	复旦大学数学科学学院
黄云敏	复旦大学数学科学学院
陈冬梅	复旦大学经济学院风险管理与保险学系
段白鸽	复旦大学经济学院风险管理与保险学系
黄　煜	复旦大学经济学院风险管理与保险学系
林　琳	复旦大学经济学院风险管理与保险学系
楼平易	复旦大学经济学院风险管理与保险学系
沈　婷	复旦大学经济学院风险管理与保险学系
钱　勇	复旦大学经济学院风险管理与保险学系
张仕英	复旦大学经济学院风险管理与保险学系
刘炳磊	复旦大学经济学院风险管理与保险学系
杨鈜毅	复旦大学经济学院风险管理与保险学系
陈羽莎	复旦大学经济学院风险管理与保险学系
瞿艺玲	复旦大学经济学院风险管理与保险学系
盘秋璇	复旦大学经济学院风险管理与保险学系
李琛淇	复旦大学经济学院风险管理与保险学系
刘招佑	复旦大学经济学院风险管理与保险学系
苏咪娅	复旦大学经济学院风险管理与保险学系
徐　炜	复旦大学中国保险科技实验室

目录

序言 ·· 6

1 教学历程与课程建设 ·· 8
Curriculum

2 研究机构 ·· 43
Research Institutes at Fudan University

3 复旦保险教育回顾 ··· 54
Review of Insurance Education at Fudan University

4 人物 ·· 81
Figures

5 复旦保险科研回顾 ··· 108
Review of Insurance Research at Fudan University

6 服务社会与行业 ··· 123
Contribution to the Society and the Insurance Industry

7 社会各界对复旦保险的寄语 ·· 151
Words from All Walks of Life to Fudan Insurance

后记 ··· 157

序　言

普天同庆，举国欢腾！在中华人民共和国成立70周年的喜庆日子里，全国各族人民、海内外中华儿女，都怀着万分喜悦的心情，为我们伟大的祖国感到无比自豪，向我们伟大的祖国表达衷心祝福。今天，我身在天安门广场观礼台，看到了习近平总书记及其他党和国家领导人，亲耳聆听了习近平总书记发表的重要讲话。在天安门城楼上，习近平总书记回顾中华人民共和国70年奋进历程，展望民族复兴的光明前景，凝聚团结奋斗的磅礴力量，振奋全体中华儿女为实现"两个一百年"奋斗目标继续奋斗！新时代中国的豪迈宣言"中国的昨天已经写在人类的史册上，中国的今天正在亿万人民手中创造，中国的明天必将更加美好"激励全体中华儿女不忘初心，艰苦奋斗！

砥砺奋进70年，艰辛探索70年，我国的保险业和中华人民共和国一起走过了70年的奋斗道路。中国现代保险事业的发展以1949年10月20日中国人民保险公司正式挂牌开业为标志，风雨如晦，历经坎坷，开拓创新，从"小"到"大"，从"弱"到"强"，终于迎来了全新面貌、全新时代！百年大计，教育为本，启蒙先行，立德树人，伴随着新中国现代保险事业的发展，我国保险高等教育体系建设亦日渐成熟。燕梳智者温故知新、初心不改、孜孜不倦，虽历经百年沧桑，但中华民族的保险教育事业得以延续。从先贤们开设保险教育课程，翻译引进保险教材，培育新中国保险人才开始，薪火相传，莘莘学子为实现中国现代保险业的复兴、改革、发展而努力奋斗！

复旦大学是我国诸多高校中最早开展现代保险教育事业的院校之一，其保险教育始于1919年（民国八年）。根据《复旦丙寅年鉴（1926年）》统计，彼时复旦大学聘任了李权时、金问洙、陈望道、周德熙等大学部教员26名。周德熙教授获得美国伊利诺伊大学商学硕士学位，被聘为复旦大学商科专任教授，讲授"保险学"等课程。至1927年（民国十六年），保险教育愈发重要，"保险学原理"成为4学分商科本科生必修课程，并新增设"火险""水险""寿险"为选修课程。此外，王效文教授（民国三十六年被聘任为复旦大学法学院法律系兼任教授)编撰并于1925年2月在商务印书馆出版的《保险学》，是我国第一部保险学专著，王效文教授亦被保险界称为"中国保险学理论研究的拓荒者"。周绍濂教授（民国三十五年被聘任为复旦大学理学院数理系专任教授）撰写了数篇保险方面的论文，并编写了《商用数学》《人寿保险计算学》等教材。

中华人民共和国成立以后，百废待兴，复旦大学档案馆收藏的成绩单显示，1949年至全国高校院系调整前，复旦大学仍然坚持开设"保险学""社会保险""劳动保险""保险合作"等6门课程。1978年改革开放后，国内保险业迅速恢复和发展，复旦大学恢复"保险学"教育，并且承办彼时国内唯一、全国首届金融管理干部专修班，为改革开放后的金融行业培养了大量金融干部。

复旦大学先贤们"博学而笃志、切问而近思"之精神代代传承，复旦保险教育事业薪火相传。20世纪90年代后，复旦保险教育发展更加朝气蓬勃、充满活力：1994年友邦－复旦精算中心成立，1996年复旦大学经济学院保险研究所成立，2002年复旦大学经济学院风险管理与保险学系成立，2013年复旦发展研究院成立中国保险与社会安全研究中心，2017年复旦大学中国保险科技实验室成立……

值此全国振奋之时，恰逢复旦保险教育百年纪念之际，受复旦保险教育事业先贤之感召，抚今追昔，深感吾辈所处大变革时代发展机遇之珍贵，继往开来！笃志推动新中国保险行业发展赤诚之心尤在，心情为之振奋！由复旦大学许闲教授组织整理复旦保险教育百年历程之照片、纪实等史料，并将其汇编成册，意义重大！兴奋之余，感慨万千，仓促下笔虽难尽本人此时此刻的心情，但有幸为画册作序，便抛砖引玉，以飨保险人。

2019年10月1日

1 / 教学历程与课程建设

复旦大学保险课程在百年的历史长河中几沐风雨，历经中华民国、中华人民共和国成立和改革开放三大时期，见证了华夏版图的沧桑变化和民族保险业的浮沉。回望百年来的课程设置变迁，无论世事盛衰，复旦保险课程教育始终筚路蓝缕，薪火不断，始终在时代的潮流中奋楫击水。踏入新百年，复旦保险课程将秉承几代师生"自强不息、与时俱进"的精神，继往开来，拥抱科技变革的浪潮，以新的姿态迈入新征程。

复旦大学保险教育最早可追溯至1919年（民国八年），彼时保险学为复旦商科本科一年级课程，至1927年（民国十六年），保险教育愈发重要，保险学原理成为4学分商科本科生必修课程，新增设课程火险、水险、寿险则为选修课程。20世纪30年代抗日战争爆发后，在艰苦条件下，复旦仍坚持保险教育，将保险学列为选修课程。1949年中华人民共和国成立后，复旦大学立即恢复保险学科教育，于当年在商学院、法学院开设保险学、社会保险等课程。改革开放后我国逐渐恢复保险业，复旦大学紧跟时代步伐，开设保险课程，并接受人民银行委托，于1982年为金融管理干部开设保险相关课程。步入新时代后，复旦大学紧跟时代潮流，所开设课程理论性与实践性兼具，并获得英国精算师协会考试豁免认证，培养了一批与国际接轨的保险业人才。

Curriculum

In the past 100 years, the insurance curriculum at Fudan University has gone through hardships and tribulations and has witnessed the vicissitudes of China's territory and the ups and downs of China's insurance industry from the Republic of China to the foundation of the People's Republic of China (PRC) and then the reform and opening up. Looking backward through the century, in spite of the huge changes in its surroundings, Fudan University has constantly been providing insurance education, which always leads the trend of the times. Entering the new century, Fudan's insurance education will adhere to the spirit of "self-improvement and advancing with the times" that generations of Fudan'ers believe, and will continue to embrace the wave of technological changes and sail another journey with a brand new attitude.

1919 (the eighth year of the Republic of China) was the first year of Fudan insurance education, when Insurance was a subject for freshmen in business school at Fudan University. In 1927 (the sixteenth year of the Republic of China), insurance education had become increasingly important with *Principles of Insurance* being a 4-credit compulsory course for business undergraduate students and newly added *Fire Insurance*, *Marine Insurance* and *Life Insurance* being elective courses. After the outbreak of the War of Resistance against Japanese Aggression in the 1930s, Fudan still persisted in insurance education and listed *Insurance* as an elective course of the Department of Statistics. After the founding of PRC in 1949, Fudan University resumed insurance education instantly and set up courses such as *Insurance* and *Social Insurance* in business school and law school that year. After starting the reform and opening up, China gradually reestablished its insurance industry while Fudan University also started to offer insurance-related courses. Entrusted by the People's Bank of China, Fudan University offered insurance-related courses for financial management cadres. After entering the new era, Fudan University keeps up with the trend of the times. The courses offered are both theoretical and practical with accreditation granted by the Institute and Faculty of Actuaries (IFoA) and have trained a group of insurance professionals who are in line with international standards.

1919年（民国八年）是复旦保险教育元年，彼时保险为商科科目。复旦大学为预科一年级和本科一年级都开设了"保险学"课程。复旦大学保险教育于此启航，为国家培养了大批保险人才。

1919 (the eighth year of the Republic of China) was the first year of Fudan insurance education, when Insurance was a business subject. Fudan University offered the course *Insurance* for both university foundation year students and freshmen. The insurance education of Fudan University set sail here and have cultivated a large number of insurance talents for the country.

1919年（民国八年）复旦大学章程，当年复旦大学为本科一年级开设"保险学"。

The Catalogue and Directory of Fudan University in 1919 (the eighth year of the Republic of China). In that year, Fudan University set up Insurance curriculum for freshmen.

Curriculum

1920年（民国九年）复旦大学修改章程，拟开设保险系，与银行系、会计系、工业管理系、国际贸易系并列，标志着复旦大学保险教育进一步深化。此时，保险学教育主要集中于进出口保险、火险和水险。同时，复旦大学提高了保险教育的全面性，开设四门课程，分别为"保险学""保险簿记""保险利息算学""保险原理"。

In 1920 (the ninth year of the Republic of China), Fudan University amended its Catalogue and Directory and proposed to establish the Insurance Department, in line with the Banking Department, the Accounting Department, the Industrial Management Department and the International Trade Department, which marked the further deepening of insurance education at Fudan University. At this time, insurance education mainly focused on import and export insurance, fire insurance and marine insurance. Meanwhile, To improve the comprehensiveness of its insurance education, Fudan University set up four courses: *Insurance Science*, *Insurance Accounting*, *Insurance Interest* and *Principles of Insurance*.

 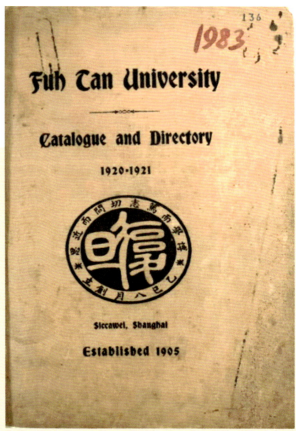

1920年复旦大学章程封面。
The cover of Catalogue and Directory of Fudan University in 1920.

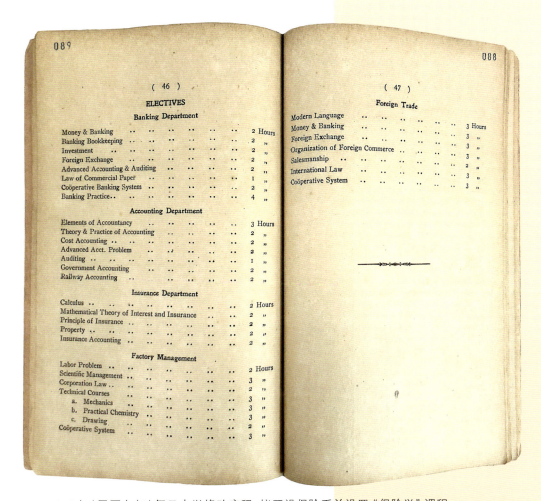

1920年（民国九年）复旦大学修改章程，拟开设保险系并设置"保险学"课程。

In 1920 (the ninth year of the Republic of China), Fudan University amended its Catalogue and Directory and proposed to establish the Insurance Department and set up Insurance courses.

1920年（民国九年）复旦大学修改章程后，对于保险课程的要求包括"进出口保险""水险""火险"等内容。

After the amendment of Fudan University Catalogue and Directory in 1920: the course *Insurance* should cover topics such as Export/Import Insurance, Marine Insurance and Fire Insurance.

1920年，复旦大学提高了保险教育的全面性，开设了四门课程，分别为"保险学""保险簿记""保险利息算学""保险原理"。

In 1920, Fudan University improved the comprehensiveness of its insurance education by offering four courses: *Insurance Science*, *Insurance Accounting*, *Insurance Interest*, and *Principles of Insurance*.

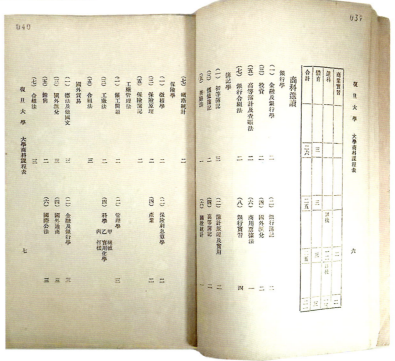

Curriculum

1927年，复旦大学修改章程，将"保险原理"设为商学院必修课程（四学分），并将"水险""火险""寿险"作为选修课，复旦保险教育从理论走向实务。

In 1927, Fudan University amended its Catalogue and Directory, setting *Principles of Insurance* as a compulsory course for business school (4 credits) and *Marine Insurance*, *Fire Insurance* and *Life Insurance* as elective courses. Fudan insurance education paid more attention to practice.

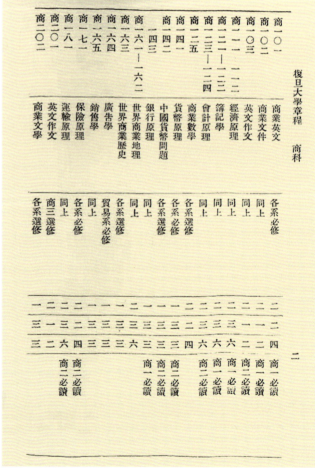

1927年（民国十六年）复旦修改章程，将"保险学原理"设为必修课（四学分），并将"水险""火险""寿险"作为选修课。

In 1927 (the sixteenth year of the Republic of China), Fudan University amended its Catalogue and Directory to make *Principles of Insurance* a compulsory course for business school (4 credits) and added *Marine Insurance*, *Fire Insurance* and *Life Insurance* as elective courses.

20世纪30年代抗日战争爆发后,复旦大学内迁重庆。在艰苦条件下,复旦大学仍坚持保险教育,将"保险学"列为统计系选修课程。

After the outbreak of the War of Resistance Against Japanese Aggression in the 1930s, Fudan University moved to Chongqing. Under the difficult conditions, Fudan University still persisted in insurance education and listed *Insurance* as an elective course in the Department of Statistics.

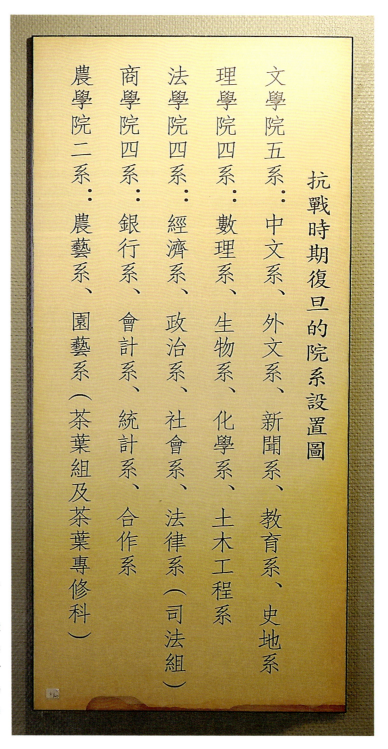

抗战时期复旦的院系设置图

文學院五系：中文系、外文系、新聞系、教育系、史地系

理學院四系：數理系、生物系、化學系、土木工程系

法學院四系：經濟系、政治系、社會系、法律系（司法組）

商學院四系：銀行系、會計系、統計系、合作系

農學院二系：農藝系、園藝系（茶葉組及茶葉專修科）

抗战时期,复旦大学商科设立银行系、会计系、统计系、合作系。

During the War of Resistance Against Japanese Aggression, the Business School of Fudan University set up four departments: the Banking Department, the Accounting Department, the Cooperation Department and the Statistics Department.

抗战时期，复旦大学在统计系下开设"保险学"选修。

During the War of Resistance Against Japanese Aggression, Fudan University introduced *Insurance* as an elective course under the Department of Statistics.

1949年中华人民共和国成立后，复旦大学立即恢复保险学科教育，于当年在商学院、法学院、财经学院开设"保险学""社会保险"等课程，为中国培养优秀保险业人才。

After the founding of the People's Republic of China in 1949, Fudan University resumed insurance education instantly and set up courses such as *Insurance* and *Social Insurance* in its Business School, Law School and School of Finance and Economics to cultivate outstanding insurance professionals for China.

1949年，复旦大学法学院社会学系开设"社会保险"课程作为三学分必修课程。

In 1949, the Sociology Department within the Law School of Fudan University introduced the course *Social Insurance* as a three-credit compulsory course.

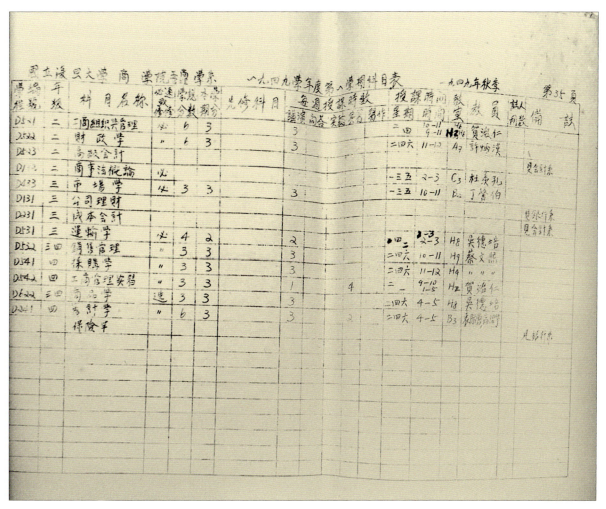

1949年,复旦大学商学院工商管理学系开设"保险学"作为三学分必修课程。

In 1949, the Department of Business Administration within the Business School of Fudan University introduced *Insurance* as a three-credit compulsory course.

1949年，复旦大学商学院银行学系开设"保险学"作为三学分必修课程。

In 1949, the Department of Banking within the Business School of Fudan University introduced *Insurance* as a three-credit compulsory course.

1949年，复旦大学商学院国际贸易系开设"保险学"作为三学分必修课程。
In 1949, the Department of International Trade within the Business School of Fudan University introduced *Insurance* as a three-credit compulsory course.

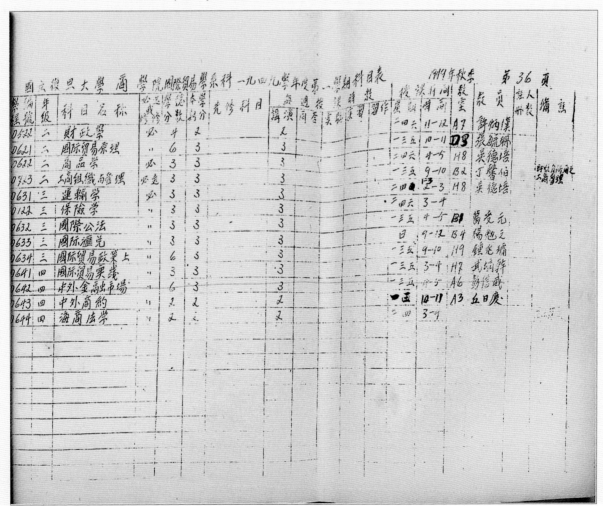

Curriculum

1949年，复旦大学商学院合作学系开设"保险合作"作为三学分必修课程。

In 1949, the Department of Cooperation within the Business School of Fudan University introduced *Insurance Cooperation* as a three-credit compulsory course.

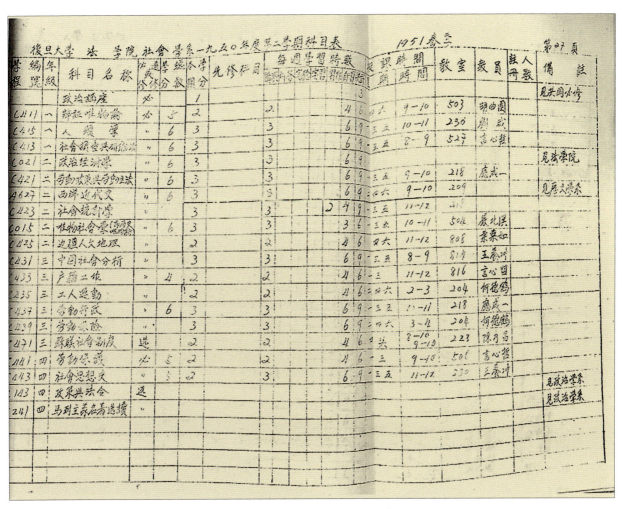

1950年，复旦大学法学院社会学系开设"劳动保险"作为三学分必修课程。

In 1950, the Sociology Department within the Law School of Fudan University introduced *Labor Insurance* as a three-credit compulsory course.

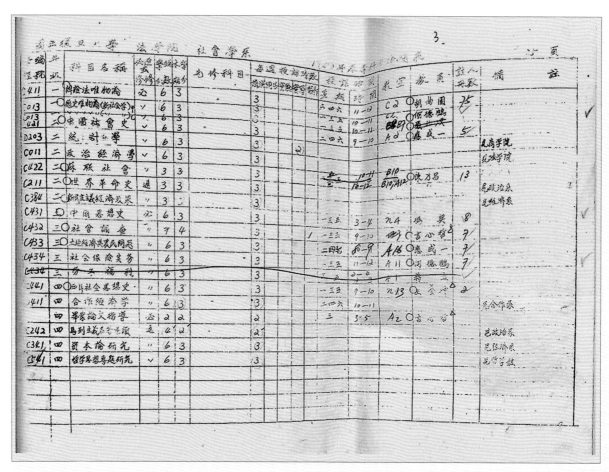

1950年，复旦大学法学院社会学系开设"社会保险实务"作为三学分必修课程。

In 1950, the Sociology Department within the Law School of Fudan University introduced *Social Insurance Practice* as a three-credit compulsory course.

1950年，复旦大学商学院国际贸易系开设"保险学"作为三学分必修课程。
In 1950, the Department of International Trade within the Business School of Fudan University introduced *Insurance* as a three-credit compulsory course.

课程编号	年级	科目名称	必选或选修	学分数	本学期分	先修科目	每周学习时数 讲演	问答	实验	实习	看作	自习	共	受课时间 星期	时间	教室	教员	註册人数	备註
D523	二	国际贸易原理	必	6	3		3					6	9	一四	11-12 10-12	542	张航珊		
D525	二	商用英文	"	4	2		2					4	6	一四	2-3	522	彭信威		
D521	二	财政学(国)	"	4	2		2					4	6	一六	9-10	222	许炳汉		
D537	三	国际贸易政策	"	6	3		3					6	9	一五	1-2, 3-4 9-10	214	锺兆璿		
D534	三	国际商法与商约	"	3	3		3					6	9	三五	10-12	202	云峻		
D538	三	保险学	"	3	3		3					6	9	三五	11-12	202			
D539	三四	国际贸易实务	"	6	3		3					6	9	二四六	10-11	803	许炳汉		
D542	四	新民主主义对外贸易政策	"	2	2		2			3	3	9		三四六	1-2 11-12	814	武靖轩		
D551	一	应用文	选	2	1		1			1	1	3		二四	4-5	805	杨范之		
D561	二	近代贸易史	"	2	2		2					4	6	三五	10-11	213	郑祖中		
D574	三四	国营贸易	"	2	2		2					4	6	二四	3-4	805	杨范之		
D575	"	中国国际贸易问题	"	3	3		3					6	9	二四六	2-3	805	"		
D576	"	贸易名著选读	"	3	3		3					6	9						
D143	"	国际金融市场	"	3	3		3					6	9	一三五	8-9		张航珊		
D581	"	贸易计划	"	2	2		2					4	6	二	8-10	211	陈谷遹		
D643	"	仓库学																	
D025		企业组织与管理												二四六	8-9	209	丁馨伯		

复旦大学商学院国际贸易学系一九五〇年度第二学期科目表　1951春季　第34页

1950年，复旦大学商学院银行学系开设"保险学"作为三学分必修课程。

In 1950, the Department of Banking within the Business School of Fudan University introduced *Insurance* as a three-credit compulsory course.

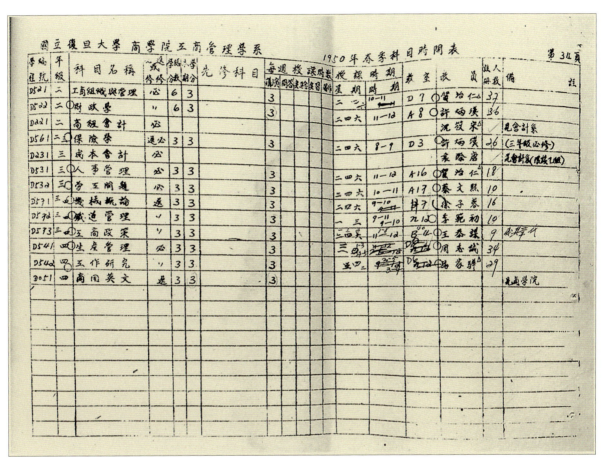

1950年,复旦大学商学院工商管理学系开设"保险学"作为三学分必修课程。

In 1950, the Department of Business Administration within the Business School of Fudan University introduced *Insurance* as a three-credit compulsory course.

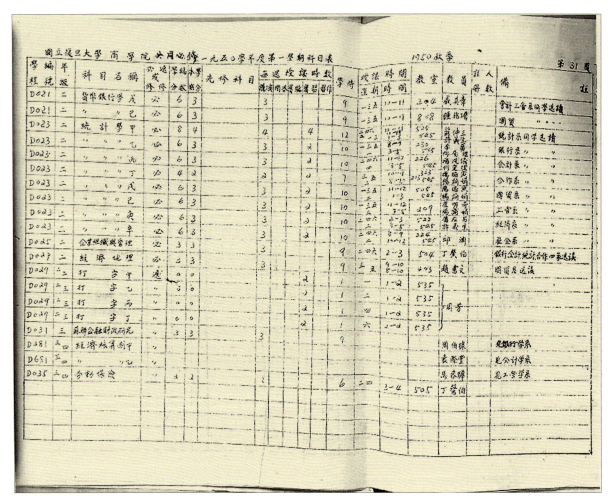

1950年,复旦大学商学院开设"劳动保险"作为三学分共同必修课程。

In 1950, Fudan University Business School introduced *Labor Insurance* as a three-credit common compulsory course.

1950年，复旦大学商学院工商管理系开设"劳动保险"作为两学分选修课程。

In 1950, the Department of Business Administration within the Business School of Fudan University introduced *Labor Insurance* as a two-credit elective course.

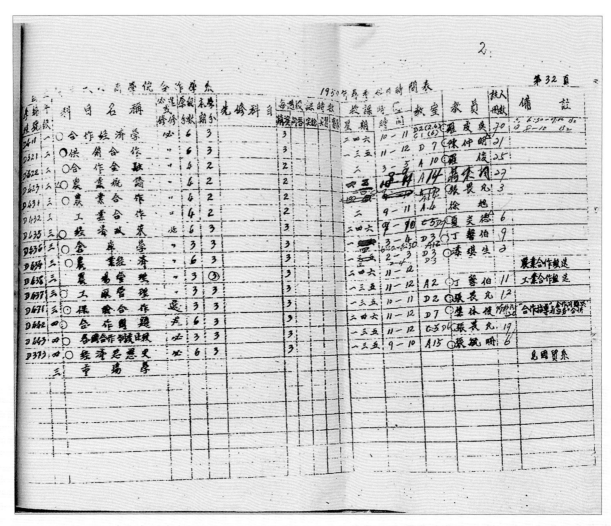

1950年，复旦大学商学院合作学系开设"保险合作"作为三学分选修课程。

In 1950, the Department of Cooperation within the Business School of Fudan University introduced *Insurance Cooperation* as a three-credit elective course.

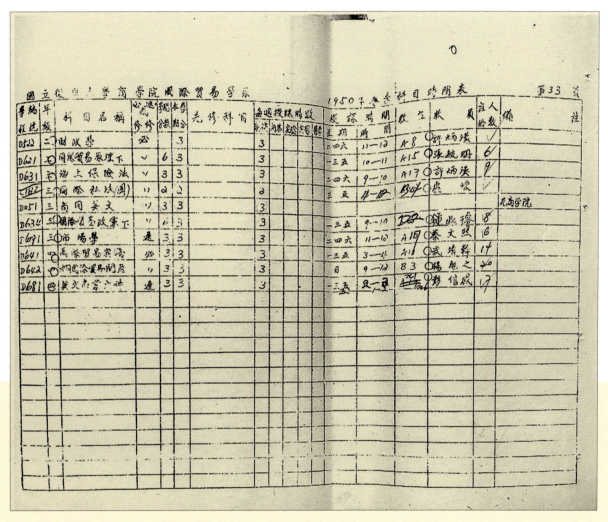

1950年，复旦大学商学院国际贸易系开设"海上保险法"作为三学分必修课程。

In 1950, the Department of International Trade within the Business School of Fudan University introduced *Marine Insurance Law* as a three-credit compulsory course.

1951年，复旦大学财经学院企业经营系开设"保险学"作为两学分必修课程。

In 1951, the Department of Business Administration within the School of Finance and Economics of Fudan University introduced *Insurance* as a two-credit compulsory course.

1951年，复旦大学财经学院银行学系开设"保险学"作为两学分必修课程。

In 1951, the Department of Banking within the School of Finance and Economics of Fudan University opened *Insurance* as a two-credit compulsory course.

1951年，复旦大学财经学院国际贸易学系开设"保险学"作为两学分必修课程。

In 1951, the Department of International Trade within the School of Finance and Economics of Fudan University introduced *Insurance* as a two-credit compulsory course.

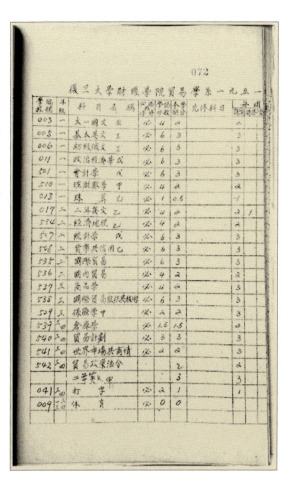

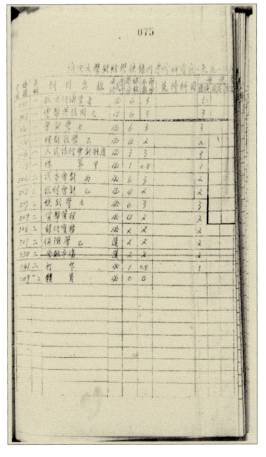

1951年，复旦大学财经学院银行学系开设"保险学"作为两学分选修课程。

In 1951, the Department of Banking within the School of Finance and Economics of Fudan University introduced *Insurance* as a two-credit elective course.

1951年，复旦大学法学院社会学系开设"劳动保险"作为三学分必修课程。

In 1951, the Sociology Department within the Law School of Fudan University introduced *Labor Insurance* as a three-credit compulsory course.

1952年院系调整后,复旦大学保险学师资划转至其他高校。

After the adjustment of faculties in 1952, the insurance faculties of Fudan University were transferred to other universities.

改革开放后我国逐渐恢复保险业,复旦大学紧跟时代步伐,开设保险课程。在全国保险业百废待兴时期,复旦大学担当起了重振中国保险业的重任,为改革开放后保险业的发展输送了大批优质人才,不仅在经济学系开设保险课程,还接受人民银行委托,为金融管理干部专修科开设保险相关课程。

After starting the reform and opening up, China gradually reestablished its insurance industry while Fudan University also followed the trend and started to offer insurance-related courses. At such a time when China needs to rebuild its insurance industry from scratch, Fudan University undertook the important task of restoring China's insurance industry and cultivated a large number of high-quality professionals for the development of insurance industry after the start of the reform and opening up. Apart from opening insurance-related courses in the Department of Economics, Fudan University, entrusted by the People's Bank of China, also offered insurance-related courses for financial management cadres.

复旦大学接受人民银行委托(自1980年起),于1982年为金融管理干部专修科开设保险相关课程。

Fudan University, entrusted by the People's Bank of China (since 1980), offered insurance courses for financial management cadres in 1982.

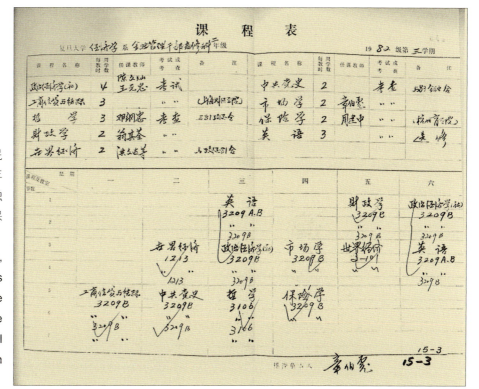

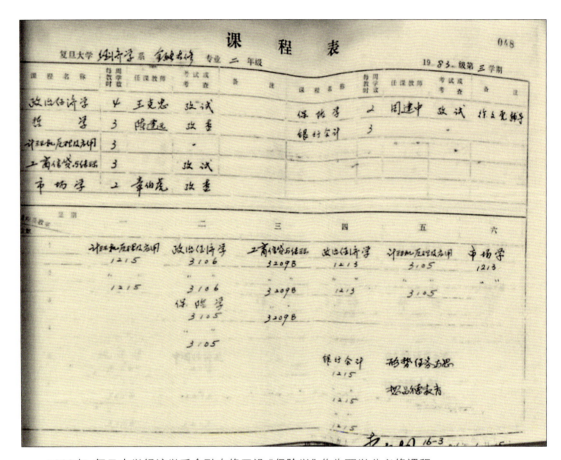

1982年，复旦大学经济学系金融专修开设"保险学"作为两学分必修课程。

In 1982, the Department of Economics of Fudan University offered *Insurance* as a two-credit compulsory course.

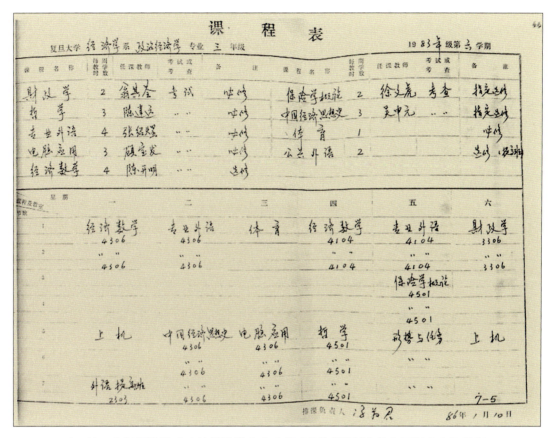

1982年,复旦大学经济学系政治经济学专业开设"保险学概论"作为两学分必修课程。

In 1982, the Department of Economics of Fudan University offered *Introduction to Insurance* as a two-credit compulsory course for students majoring in Political Economy.

1982年，复旦大学经济学系金融专业开设"保险学概论"作为两学分必修课程。

In 1982, the Department of Economics of Fudan University offered *Introduction to Insurance* as a two-credit compulsory course for students majoring in Finance.

步入新时代后，复旦大学紧跟时代潮流，所开设课程理论性与实践性兼具，并成为英国精算师协会考试豁免认证高校，培养了一批与国际接轨的保险业人才。

After entering the new era, Fudan University keeps up with the trend of the times. The courses offered are both theoretical and practical with accreditation granted by the Institute and Faculty of Actuaries (IFoA) and have trained a group of insurance professionals who are in line with international standards.

2019版保险本科生培养计划，经济学通识教育与保险专业教育并重。

The 2019 edition of undergraduates education plan, which pays attention to both basic economic senses and professional insurance education.

（三）多元发展路径课程

多元发展包括专业进阶（含荣誉项目）、跨学科发展（含辅修学士学位项目）和创新创业等不同路径，要求在院系专业导师指导下选择其中一条发展路径，按路径要求修读课程。总平均绩点在3.3及以上方可修读荣誉课程。

1. 专业进阶路径

修满36学分。其中专业进阶I组中A组必修9学分和B组至少修读11学分。修读专业进阶路径的学生，可以向经济学院申请推免直研资格，毕业时获得保险学专业毕业证书及学士学位证书。

专业进阶模块课程设置如下：

（1）专业进阶模块（33学分）

		课程名称	课程代码	学分	周学时	含实践学分	开课学期	备注	
专业进阶I组（至少修读20学分）	A组（必修9学分）	精算数学	ECON130235	3	3	1	5	CM1课程（IFoA）	
		财产与责任保险	ECON130234	3	3		5		
		风险理论与精算建模	ECON130233	3	3	1	6	CS2课程（IFoA）	
	B组（至少修读11学分）	保险公司财务管理	ECON130167	2	2	1	5	VEE课程（SOA）	精算与风险管理（至少修读一门）
		企业风险管理	ECON130236	2	2	1	7	VEE课程（SOA）	
		金融工程与损失准备金	ECON130238	3	3	1	7	CM2课程（IFoA）	
		保险科技	ECON115005	2	2		3		保险与金融模块（至少修读一门）
		海上保险	ECON130091	2	2		4		
		保险法	ECON130094	2	2	1	5		
		国际金融	ECON130003	3	3		5		
		再保险	ECON130092	2	2		6		
		社会保险比较研究	ECON130093	2	2		6		
		国际风险与保险研究	ECON130237	2	2		7		
		时间序列分析方法	ECON130083	3	3	1	春秋	方法模块（至少修读一门）	
		截面与面板数据分析	ECON130188	3	3	2	春秋		
		数量分析软件应用	ECON130189	3	3	3	春秋		
专业进阶II组（选修）（0-13学分）	A组课程	学院其他专业培养方案中的专业教育课程（含荣誉课程和UIPE项目课程）							
	B组专硕课程	经济学分析与应用（G）		3	3			限推免资产评估方向硕士	
		公司金融学（G）		3	3				
		税收理论与政策（G）		3	3			限推免税务方向硕士	
		税收筹划（G）		3	3				
		经济学分析与应用（G）		3	3			限推免国际商务方向硕士	
		国际商务（G）		3	3				
		保险学研究（G）		3	3			限推免保险方向硕士	
		保险数理基础（G）		3	3				
		公司金融学（G）		3	3			限推免金融方向硕士	
		金融机构与市场（G）		3	3				
	C组学硕课程	中级政治经济学（G）		3	3				
		中级宏观经济学（G）		3	3				
		中级微观经济学（G）		3	3				
		中级计量经济学（G）		3	3				
	D组硕博课程	高级微观经济学（G）		3	3				
		高级宏观经济学（G）		3	3				
		高级计量经济学（G）		3	3				

目前，复旦大学保险本科教育为学生提供多元发展路径。

At present, undergraduate insurance education at Fudan University provides students with multiple development paths.

课程类别	课程代码	课程	开课院系	学时
政治理论课	001	政治理论课 查看	000 研究生院	--
第一外国语课	002	第一外国语 查看	000 研究生院	--
第一外国语课	ECON620065	金融英语	068 经济学院	54
学位基础课	ECON630156	保险法	068 经济学院	36
	MI620002	风险管理研究	068 经济学院	36
	MI620004	保险财务分析与管理	068 经济学院	36
	MI620005	保险数理基础	068 经济学院	36
	MI620017	保险学研究	068 经济学院	36
	MI620020	经济学(CB2)	068 经济学院	36
学位专业课	MI620003	财产与责任保险	068 经济学院	36
	MI620016	保险经济学前沿专题	068 经济学院	36
	MI620018	风险理论与精算建模	068 经济学院	36
	MI620019	精算数学(CM1)	068 经济学院	36
	MI630011	公司金融学(CB1)	068 经济学院	36
	MI630013	金融工程与损失准备金(CM2)	068 经济学院	36
学位专业课	ECON620097	经济伦理学	068 经济学院	36
专业选修课	ECON620101	经济与金融的法律基础	068 经济学院	54
专业选修课	ECON630048	社会保障专题	068 经济学院	36
专业选修课	ECON630139	灾害经济学	068 经济学院	36
专业选修课	ECON630190	绿色金融理论与实务	068 经济学院	36
专业选修课	MI630001	再保险	068 经济学院	36
专业选修课	MI630005	不确定性经济学	068 经济学院	36
专业选修课	MI630010	保险科技	068 经济学院	36
专业选修课	MI630012	国际保险研究	068 经济学院	36
公共选修课	003	公共选修课 查看	000 研究生院	--

2019级保险专硕课程表，新增"经济学""公司金融学""金融工程与损失准备金""保险科技"等课程。

In the curriculum of Insurance Professional Master's Degree Program in 2019, more courses were offered such as *Economics*, *Corporate Finance*, *Finance Engineering and Reserves*, and *InsurTech*.

2019年9月，复旦大学正式成为英国精算师协会（IFoA）考试豁免认证高校。复旦大学也是目前中国大陆唯一一所首次递交申请，即获得全部6门核心课程（Core Principles）考试豁免的综合性高校。

In September 2019, Fudan University officially became a university with IFoA exemption accreditation. Fudan University is also the only comprehensive university in China's mainland to be granted exemption from all six Core Principles examinations at its first application.

Research Institutes at Fudan University

With a long history and a strong academic background in insurance, different departments of Fudan University have established insurance research institutes, including but not limited to: AXA-NMU Fudan Insurance Research Center, Fudan Insurance Research Institute, AIA-Fudan Actuarial Center, Shanghai Insurance Development Planning Project Research Office, the Department of Risk Management and Insurance in the School of Economics, China Insurance and Social Security Research Center, China InsurTech Laboratory of Fudan University, etc.

2 / 研究机构

复旦大学保险教育历史悠久，保险教研学术力量雄厚，复旦大学不同院系相继成立保险研究机构，包括并不限于：安盛/国卫-复旦保险研究中心、复旦大学保险研究所、友邦-复旦精算中心、上海市保险发展规划项目研究室、复旦大学经济学院风险管理与保险学系、复旦大学中国保险与社会安全研究中心、复旦大学中国保险科技实验室等。

1996年，安盛/国卫-复旦保险研究中心成立。
The establishment of AXA-NMU Fudan Insurance Research Center in 1996.

復旦大學

关于成立"上海市保险发展规划项目研究室"的报告

经济学院转校领导：

我中心应中国保险监督管理委员会上海办公室的要求，将于6月30日举行预备会议，讨论"上海市保险发展规划项目研究室"筹备事宜。研究室的任务是研究制订上海市保险业发展的"十五"规划和中长期规划。研究室邀请上海市副秘书长李关良、金融工委书记杨定华、复旦大学党委书记秦绍德、原上海人民银行行长龚浩成担任高级顾问，主任由上海保监办主任周延礼担任，副主任由我校保险研究所常务副所长徐文虎担任。研究室下设两个组：专家咨询组和研究组。专家咨询组集中了中外保险公司的董事长和总经理，研究组集中了复旦大学、上海交大、华东师大、上海财大等学校保险方面的研究力量，是全市性的保险学术研究机构。挂靠在经济学院300号，研究室将促进上海保险市场的发展，进一步提高复旦大学的声誉，推动保险的教学和科研。研究室经费由中外保险公司提供资助，在复旦大学设立专户，专款专用。预计研究室8月初在复旦大学挂牌。

以上报告当否，请批示。

附筹备组报告

安盛·国卫—复旦保险研究中心
2000年6月28日

2000年，上海市保险发展规划项目研究室成立。

The establishment of Shanghai Insurance Development Planning Project Research Office in 2000.

2002年，复旦大学保险研究所申请成立组建研究所理事会获批。
The approval for the establishment of the Research Institute Council in Fudan Insurance Research Institute in 2002.

安盛/国卫-复旦保险研究中心、复旦大学保险研究所、上海市保险发展规划项目研究室等保险研究机构的主要参与者与负责人为徐文虎教授。

Professor Xu Wenhu is the director of the insurance research institutions including AXA-NMU Fudan Insurance Research Center, Fudan Insurance Research Institute, and Shanghai Insurance Development Planning Project Research Office.

徐文虎

复旦大学保险系创设者,首任系主任(2002—2010年),曾任上海市法制办专家组成员、上海市保险规划项目研究室副主任、中国保险学会理事。著作有《中国保险百科全书》《保险学》等20余本,承担了多项原中国保监会和上海市政府的保险研究项目。

Xu Wenhu

Xu Wenhu is the founder of the Department of Insurance of Fudan University and the first director of the Department (from 2002 to 2010). Xu Wenhu used to be a member of the expert group at the Shanghai Legal Affairs Office, deputy director of Shanghai Insurance Development Planning Project Research Office, and director of the Insurance Institute of China. He has written more than 20 books such as *Encyclopedia of Insurance in China* and *Insurance*. He has also undertaken lots of important insurance research projects for the former China Insurance Regulatory Commission and the Shanghai municipal government.

1994年,友邦-复旦精算中心成立,中心主任为尚汉冀教授。

The year of 1994 witnessed the establishment of AIA-Fudan Actuarial Center. The director of the center is Professor Shang Hanji.

尚汉冀，男，1937年6月生于天津，祖籍浙江平湖。1960年复旦大学数学系本科毕业，1963年复旦大学微分方程研究生毕业。1964年起在复旦大学数学系任教，历任助教、讲师、副教授、教授及应用数学教研室主任等。1986—1987年曾在美国佛罗里达大学进修及合作研究。

尚教授的专长为应用数学，1993年后主要从事精算教学与研究，现任友邦-复旦精算中心主任。曾出版英文专著1部，中文著作及译作9部，发表论文70余篇。

2019年获中共中央、国务院、中央军委颁发的庆祝中华人民共和国成立70周年纪念章。

Shang Hanji

Born in Tianjin in June 1937, Shang is originally from Pinghu, Zhejiang Province. He graduated from Fudan University with an undergraduate degree in Mathematics in 1960, and received his master's degree in Differential Equations from Fudan University in 1963. Since 1964, he has been teaching in the Department of Mathematics at Fudan University and has served as a teaching assistant, lecturer, associate professor, professor and director of the Applied Mathematics Department. From 1986 to 1987, he studied at the University of Florida in the United States.

Shang is specialized in applied mathematics. Since 1993, he has been mostly engaged in teaching and doing research in actuarial science. He is now director of the AIA-Fudan Actuarial Center. He has published one monograph in English, nine books and translations in Chinese, and more than 70 papers.

In 2019, he was awarded a commemorative medal of celebrating the 70th anniversary of the founding of the People's Republic of China by the Central Committee of the Communist Party of China, the State Council and the Central Military Commission.

贺　信

复旦大学：

　　欣悉复旦大学保险系成立，我谨代表中国保险监督管理委员会表示衷心的祝贺！

　　随着我国加入WTO和保险市场的进一步对外开放，我国保险业已经步入一个新的发展时期，保险人才短缺的矛盾越来越突出。复旦大学保险系的成立，对加快保险人才培养、强化保险研究具有重要意义。希望复旦大学保险系坚持高起点、高标准，培养高素质的保险专业人才，为我国保险事业的持续快速健康发展作出积极贡献！

02.9.6

2002年复旦大学经济学院成立保险系，原中国保监会首任主席马永伟先生来信祝贺。
Mr. Ma Yongwei, the first chairman of the former China Insurance Regulatory Commission, congratulated Fudan University on establishing its Department of Insurance in 2002.

复旦大学办公室文件

校批字〔2013〕105 号

关于成立复旦大学中国保险与社会安全研究中心的批复

文科科研处：

你处报送发展研究院关于申请成立复旦大学中国保险与社会安全研究中心的请示已收悉。经研究，决定同意成立复旦大学中国保险与社会安全研究中心，隶属发展研究院，中心负责人为许闲。

特此批复

复旦大学办公室
2013 年 6 月 13 日

— 1 —

2013年，复旦大学中国保险与社会安全研究中心成立。
The year of 2013 witnessed the establishment of the China Insurance and Social Security Research Center at Fudan University.

2017年，复旦大学成立中国保险科技实验室。
Fudan University established the China InsurTech Laboratory in 2017.

许闲

复旦大学风险管理与保险学系现任主任（2018年至今）、中国保险与社会安全研究中心主任、中国保险科技实验室主任。他曾获得复旦大学卓学计划、上海市浦江人才、英国科学院牛顿高级学者等人才计划支持。许闲在国内权威杂志《金融研究》《会计研究》《国际问题研究》《数理经济技术经济研究》《财经研究》和《保险研究》等期刊发表论文超过20篇，英文成果发表于 Journal of Banking and Finance, Scandinavian Actuarial Journal, The Geneva Papers on Risk and Insurance, Disaster Prevention and Management 等重要金融保险类SSCI期刊（8篇）。许闲还主持了联合国开发计划署、英国科学院、中国国家自然科学基金项目和多项省部级（教育部、民政部、银保监会、上海市政府等）重点研究项目，多项政策建议被国家相关部门采纳。

Xu Xian

Xu Xian is the current director of the Department of Risk Management and Insurance at Fudan University (from 2018 to present), director of the China Insurance and Social Security Research Center and director of the China Insurtech Laboratory. Xu has been supported by many talent programs such as the Newton Advanced Fellowship of the British Academy, Shanghai Pujiang Program, and Fudan Zhuoxue Program. He has already published numerous papers in both international and Chinese journals, including among others *Journal of Banking and Finance, Scandinavian Actuarial Journal, The Geneva Papers on Risk and Insurance, Disaster Prevention and Management*. He has been in charge of many research projects supported by the United Nations Development Programme, the British Academy, the National Natural Science Foundation of China, the National Disaster Reduction Center of China, the Ministry of Education of the People's Republic of China, the China Insurance Regulatory Commission, etc.

3 / 复旦保险教育回顾

复旦大学保险学科的师生在多年科教活动中,积累下了一大批重要的保险教研资料,为中国保险提供了重要的学术支持。

Review of Insurance Education at Fudan University

Through years of research and education, faculties and students of Fudan Insurance have accumulated a large number of academic achievements, providing essential academic support for the insurance industry in China.

复旦大学部分保险资料。
Some insurance materials at Fudan University.

我国最早的保险教材，1925年出版，分为寿险、水险、火险、法律四编，由王效文编撰，马寅初评论为"吾国向无所谓保险学，有之，自本书始"。

The earliest insurance textbook in China was published in 1925 with four parts: Life Insurance, Marine Insurance, Fire Insurance, and Insurance Law. It was compiled by Wang Xiaowen. Ma Yinchu commented that "[t]here is no insurance in our country until this book is published."

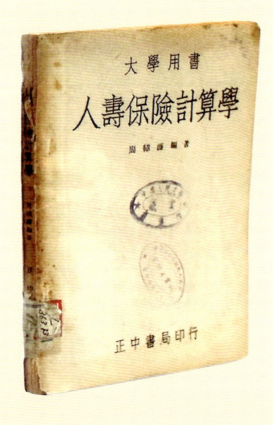

中华人民共和国成立前，复旦大学周绍濂老师编撰的保险教材《人寿保险计算学》，1946年出版，正中书局"大学用书"系列之一。其内容分为死亡表、年金、纯保险费、均衡纯准备金、近代准备金制。

The insurance textbook *Life Insurance Computing*, compiled by Professor Zhou Shaolian at Fudan University before the foundation of the People's Republic of China, was published in 1946 and listed as one of the "University Books" series of Zhengzhong Book Company. This textbook consisted of death table, annuity, net premium, balanced pure reserve and modern reserve system.

中国人民保险公司与复旦大学共同培养保险高级管理干部,第一期。
The first seminar jointly held by the People's Insurance Company of China (PICC) and Fudan University to train insurance senior management cadres.

中国人民保险公司与复旦大学共同培养保险高级管理干部，第二期。

The second seminar jointly held by PICC and Fudan University to train insurance senior management cadres.

1993年复旦大学精算教育招生广告。
Admission advertisement for actuarial education at Fudan University in 1993.

友邦-复旦精算中心教学实景。
The teaching environment at AIA-Fudan Actuarial Center.

1995年，复旦大学数学系与中国人民保险公司上海分公司合作翻译北美精算师协会准精算师课程教材正式出版，为国内第一套精算丛书。

In 1995, the Department of Mathematics of Fudan University and the Shanghai Branch of the People's Insurance Company of China jointly published the Chinese version of the actuarial course materials of the Society of Actuaries (SOA), which were the first set of actuarial books in China.

复旦大学校友薄卫民在1995年5月到1998年期间用约3年半时间内通过了北美精算学会考试，成为中国大陆第一位北美精算师。

Bo Weimin, an alumnus of Fudan University, was the first Fellow of the Society of Actuaries (FSA) from China's mainland after he passed all the exams required by SOA within 3 years and a half from May 1995 to 1998.

在精算师极为紧缺的20世纪90年代，复旦大学为上海市乃至全国培养了大批精算师。

In the 1990s when actuaries were extremely scarce, Fudan University trained a large number of actuaries for Shanghai and even the whole country.

1996年，纽约人寿为复旦大学保险学科设立奖学金。右为复旦大学原副校长徐明稚。

In 1996, New York Life Insurance Company endowed scholarships for insurance education at Fudan University. On the right stood Xu Mingzhi, former vice president of Fudan University.

国泰人寿自1996年起为复旦大学设立奖学金,迄今已22年。右为复旦大学原副校长施岳群。
Cathay Life Insurance has endowed scholarships for Fudan University for 22 consecutive years since 1996. On the right stood Shi Yuequn, former vice president of Fudan University.

2018年国泰奖学金颁奖仪式在复旦大学经济学院举行。
The 2018 Cathay Life Insurance Scholarship was awarded at the School of Economics of Fudan University.

1997年,大都会人寿保险公司与复旦大学签署合作协议,共同开展富裕性疾病调查。

In 1997, Metropolitan Life Insurance Company signed a cooperation agreement with Fudan University to jointly carry out a survey on affluenza.

近年来，复旦保险教师们也频出佳作，为保险教育做出了卓越的贡献。

In recent years, the insurance faculty at Fudan University have also published outstanding works, making great contributions to insurance education and research.

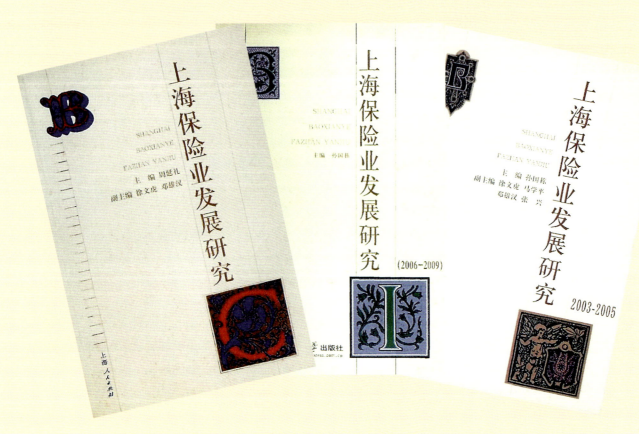

徐文虎教授主持编撰"上海保险业发展研究系列书籍"（2003年起）。
Professor Xu Wenhu has been in charge of the compilation of a series of books titled *Research of Development of Insurance Industry in Shanghai* (since 2003).

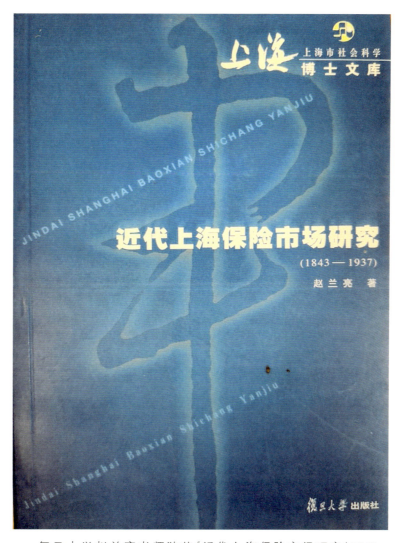

复旦大学赵兰亮老师独著《近代上海保险市场研究(1843—1937)》(2003年出版)。

Research on Modern Shanghai Insurance Market (1843-1937) by Zhao Lanliang from Fudan University (published in 2003).

徐文虎教授与陈冬梅老师共同主编《保险学》(左2004年版,右2014年第二版)。

Professor Xu Wenhu and Chen Dongmei jointly compiled *Insurance* (on the left the 2004 edition and on the right the 2nd edition in 2014).

徐文虎教授独著《中国保险市场转型研究》(2005年12月出版)。
Professor Xu Wenhu's *Research on China's Insurance Market Transformation* (2005.12).

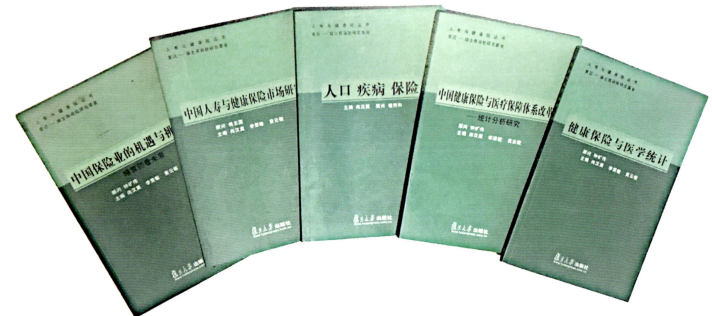

由复旦-瑞士再保险研究基金资助出版,复旦大学尚汉冀教授等共同编撰的"人寿与健康险丛书"(出版时间从左到右为:2006年、2010年、2003年、2008年、2007年)。

Funded by the Fudan-Swiss Reinsurance Research Funds, Professor Shang Hanji and his colleagues from Fudan University published the Life & Health Insurance Series (publishing time from left to right: 2006, 2010, 2003, 2008, 2007).

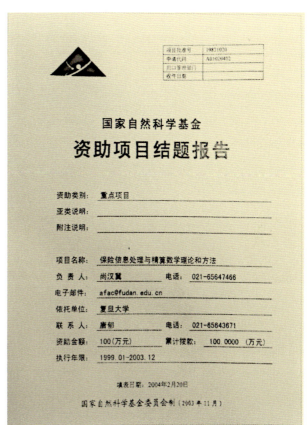

2006年，国家自然科学基金资助了第一个精算学重点项目："保险信息处理与精算数学理论和方法"，英文专著《精算学：理论与方法》出版。它是复旦大学尚汉冀教授同多所高校教授专家联合取得成就的总结。

In 2006, in the context of the first key project "Insurance Information Processing and Actuarial Mathematical Theory and Methodology" funded by the National Natural Science Foundation of China, the English monograph *Actuarial Science: Theory and Methodology* was published as a summary of the achievements of Professor Shang Hanji from Fudan University and some professors from other universities.

复旦大学保险校友裴光与徐文虎教授编著《中国保险业标准化理论研究》(2008.1)。

Research on the Theory of Insurance Standardization in China with the contribution of Professor Xu Wenhu and Fudan alumnus Pei Guang (2008.1).

2009年,复旦大学教授尚汉冀和新华医院老年医学科主任医师段俊丽教授联合主编的《老年人群疾病与医疗保障》出版,成为精算、医学跨界合作、共同应对老龄化问题的有效探索。

In 2009, Professor Shang Hanji from Fudan University and Professor Duan Junli, the chief physician of the Department of Geriatrics at Xinhua Hospital, jointly published *Diseases and Medical Security for the Elderly*, which became an effective exploration of actuarial and medical cross-border cooperation to cope with the problem of an aging population.

复旦大学保险校友裴光与徐文虎教授共同编著《中国健康保险统计制度研究》(2009.5)。
Professor Xu Wenhu and Fudan alumnus Pei Guang jointly compiled *Research on China's Insurance Statistics System* (2009.5).

丁纯教授独著《世界主要医疗保障制度模式绩效比较》(2009年第二版)。
Comparison of Performance of the World's Major Medical Security Systems and Models by Professor Ding Chun (the second edition published in 2009).

丁纯教授主编《老年人护理与护理保险》(2010.12)。

Care and Care Insurance for the Elderly co-edited by Professor Ding Chun (2010.12).

沈婷老师编著的《国际保险》被纳入"经济学新视野本科教材系列"中(2010)。

International Insurance compiled by Shen Ting has been listed in the series of "Undergraduate Textbooks in the New Horizon of Economics" (2010).

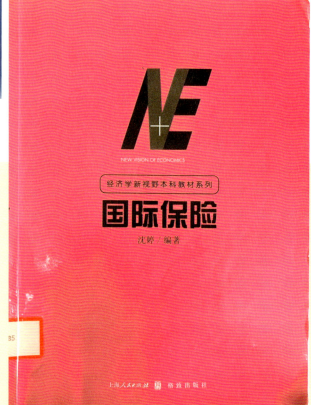

2012年，复旦大学尚汉冀教授、李荣敏老师、黄云敏老师参与编撰的"复旦-韬睿惠悦精算科学丛书"《精算学》出版。

In 2012, Professor Shang Hanji, Li Rongmin and Huang Yunmin from Fudan University participated in the compilation of *Actuarial Science*, a book in the Fudan-Towers Watson Actuarial Science series.

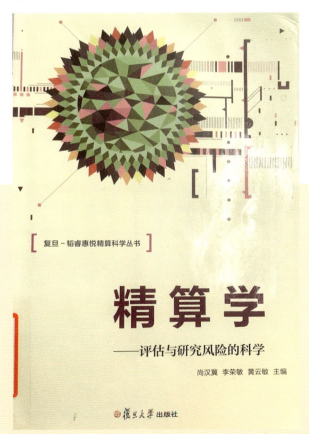

2013年，段白鸽老师参与编著的《非寿险索赔准备金评估：随机性方法》出版。

In 2013, Duan Baige participated in the compilation and publication of *Evaluation of Non-life Insurance Claims Reserve: Stochastic Method*.

徐文虎教授与陈冬梅老师共同编著"泛海书院丛书"《中国保险业后发优势探索》（2015.12）。

Professor Xu Wenhu and Chen Dongmei jointly published *Exploration of the Second-mover Advantages of China's Insurance Industry*, which was listed in the Fanhai College Book Series (2015.12).

《闲话保险：十年变迁(2007—2016)》是许闲教授十年以来有关保险的随笔结集成册(2017.10)。

Gossip Insurance: the Changes in Last Ten Years (2007—2016) is a book of essays on insurance by Professor Xu Xian (2017.10).

复旦大学风险管理与保险学系身处中国保险科技学术研究前沿，为行业发展提供重要支持。

The Department of Risk Management and Insurance at Fudan University stands at the forefront of the academic research on insurance science and technology in China and provides important support for the development of the insurance industry.

2018年1月，段白鸽老师独著的《非寿险索赔准备金评估：统计模型与方法》出版，提升了我国非寿险精算学科的统计分析体系。

In January 2018, Duan Baige's *Evaluation of Non-life Insurance Claims Reserve: Statistical Models and Methods* was published, which improved the statistical analysis system of the non-life insurance actuarial discipline in China.

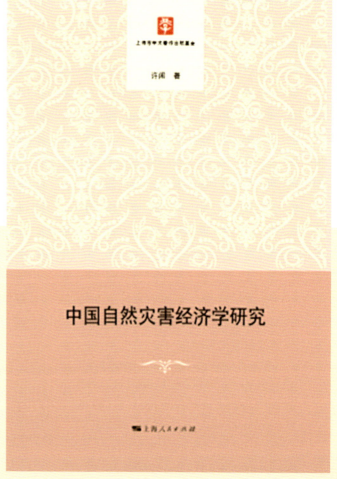

许闲教授独著的《中国自然灾害经济学研究》是国内极少的研究自然灾害经济学专著（2018.8）。

Professor Xu Xian's *Research on Natural Disasters Economics in China* is a rare monograph on economics of natural disasters in China (2018.8).

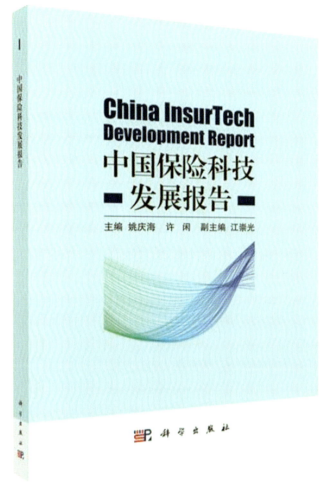

许闲教授主编《中国保险科技发展报告》（2018.10）。

China InsurTech Development Report co-edited by Professor Xu Xian (2018.10).

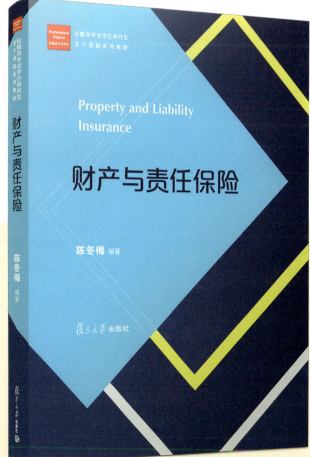

陈冬梅老师编著的"经管类专业学位研究生主干课程系列教材"《财产与责任保险》（2019.4）。

Property and Liability Insurance compiled by Chen Dongmei as a textbook for the Professional Master's Degree Program in Economic Management (2019.4).

许闲教授独著的"纪念改革开放四十周年丛书"《保险大国崛起：中国模式》(2019.5)。

The Rise of Insurance Powers: The Chinese Model written by Professor Xu Xian for the Commemoration of 40th Anniversary of Reform and Opening Up Series (2019.5).

4 / 人物

Figures

Throughout the century of insurance education at Fudan University, a large number of dedicated teachers passed their insurance knowledge from generation to generation. The history can be traced back to Mr. Zhou Dexi, Mr. Wang Xiaowen and Mr. Zhou Shaolian before the foundation of the People's Republic of China. Since then, a number of insurance teachers at Fudan University passed the torch of insurance education and worked relentlessly to train batches of insurance professionals. For example, since the establishment of AIA-Fudan Actuarial Centre in 1994, hundreds of students have completed their actuarial studies here and become qualified actuaries to serve the society. Besides, the School of Economics of Fudan University officially established the Department of Insurance in 2002. Students who graduated from the Department of Risk Management and Insurance within the School of Economics at Fudan University are growing to become the mainstay of China's insurance industry.

Meanwhile, Fudan University has actively provided education service for the country and the society, including but not limited to training financial cadres for the People's Bank of China, running schools jointly with China Pacific Insurance Company, and cultivating students jointly with Feng Chia University in Taiwan, China.

百年复旦大学保险教育，一大批辛勤教学的教师薪火相传，传授保险知识。信史可追溯至中华人民共和国成立前的周德熙先生、王效文先生、周绍濂先生……在此之后，一位位复旦保险教师传递保险教育火炬，孜孜不倦地培养了一批又一批保险人才：友邦-复旦精算中心于1994年成立以来，已为社会培养了一大批精算师。2002年，复旦大学经济学院正式成立保险系（之后更名为复旦大学风险管理与保险学系）。毕业于复旦大学经济学院风险管理与保险学系的学生们，正成长为保险业的中流砥柱。

除此之外，复旦大学还积极为国家和社会提供教育服务，包括并不限于：为中国人民银行培养金融干部、与太平洋保险公司联合办学、与中国台湾逢甲大学联合培养学生等。

以下图片按时间顺序排列。

The photos below are listed in chronological order.

周德熙

复旦大学保险学、银行学、商业地理教授，银行系系主任。根据复旦丙寅年鉴（1926年），26位商科教员中，13位具备海外名校学历背景。周德熙教授就是其中之一，他于美国伊利诺伊大学商学硕士毕业后，在复旦大学开设了保险学课程，为复旦大学保险教育奠定基石。

Zhou Dexi was a professor of insurance, banking, and business geography at Fudan University and dean of the Department of Banking. According to the Fudan University Yearbook of Bingyin Year (1926), 13 out of the 26 teachers in Business School had received education from overseas universities. Professor Zhou Dexi was one of them. After graduating from the University of Illinois with a master's degree in business, he introduced the course *Insurance* to Fudan University, which laid the foundation for the insurance education at Fudan University.

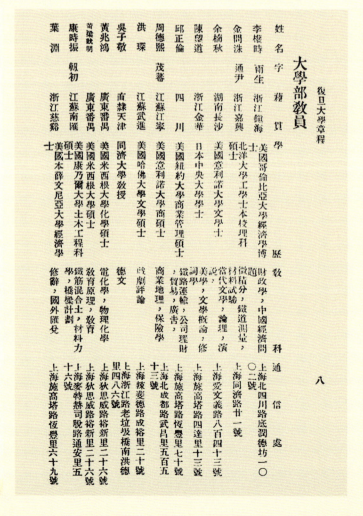

王效文

复旦大学教授，保险界称其为"中国保险学理论研究的拓荒者"。他于1925年2月在商务印书馆出版的《保险学》是我国第一部保险学专著。该书共分寿险、水险、火险和法律四编。《保险学》出版后，在保险界引起很大反响：各人学商科纷纷采用它作为教材，其受欢迎程度和社会影响不言而喻。

Wang Xiaowen, a professor at Fudan University, was known as "the pioneer in theoretical research on insurance in China". Published in February 1925 by the Commercial Press, *Insurance* was the first monograph on insurance in China. The book was divided into four parts: Life Insurance, Marine Insurance, Fire Insurance, and Insurance Law. Its publication evoked great repercussions in the insurance field. Business departments in various universities adopted it as a textbook. There was no doubt in its popularity and social influence.

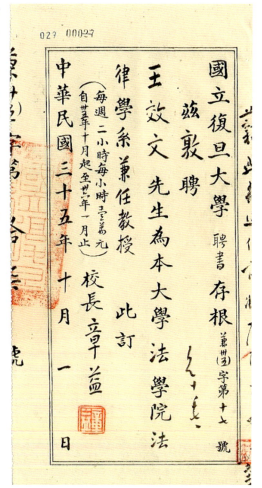

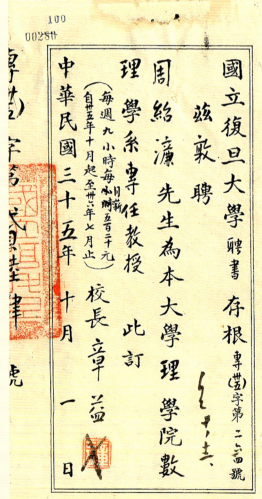

周绍濂

复旦大学理学院数学系专任教授。1933年初,周绍濂进入巴黎大学专攻数学,成为我国最早出国深造的研究生之一。1947年,周绍濂应聘兼任上海商业专科学校校长。为此,他还撰写了数篇经济方面的论文,并编写了《商用数学》《人寿保险计算学》等教材。1955年,复旦大学决定派朱子清、周绍濂等7人支持兰州大学。

Zhou Shaolian was a full-time professor in the Department of Mathematics in the Faculty of Science at Fudan University. In early 1933, Zhou Shaolian was admitted into Paris University for mathematics and became one of the earliest overseas postgraduate students from China. In 1947, Zhou Shaolian was appointed President of Shanghai Commercial College. He also published several economic papers and compiled textbooks such as *Commercial Mathematics* and *Life Insurance Computing*. In 1955, Fudan University decided to send seven people, among whom were Zhu Ziqing and Zhou Shaolian, to support Lanzhou University.

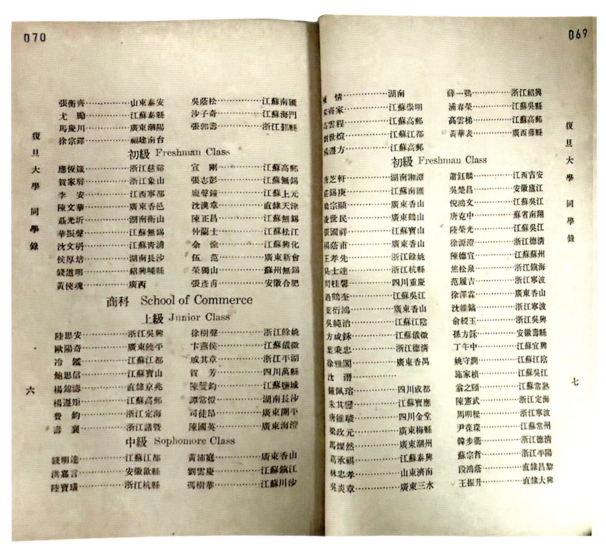

1920年复旦大学商科同学录。
Alumni Page of the Business School of Fudan University in 1920.

1984年首届金融管理干部专修班毕业合影。
Graduation photo of the First Financial Management Cadres Training Class in 1984.

1996年,友邦-复旦精算中心第一期培训举办毕业典礼。
In 1996, AIA-Fudan Actuarial Centre held the graduation ceremony for the first training program.

1997年,复旦大学经济学院与数学系老师共同参观澳大利亚国卫保险。

In 1997, faculties from the School of Economics and the Department of Mathematics of Fudan University visited NMU Insurance Group together.

2004年,友邦-复旦精算中心十周年庆典。

In 2004, the AIA-Fudan Actuarial Center celebrated its 10th anniversary.

2007年复旦大学保险系本科生毕业照。

Graduation photo of the undergraduates in the Department of Insurance of Fudan University in 2007.

2007年复旦大学保险系硕士生毕业照。
Graduation photo of the graduates in the Department of Insurance of Fudan University in 2007.

2009年复旦大学保险系本科生毕业照。
Graduation photo of the undergraduates in the Department of Insurance of Fudan University in 2009.

2009年复旦大学保险系硕士生毕业照。
Graduation photo of the graduates in the Department of Insurance of Fudan University in 2009.

2010年复旦大学保险系本科生毕业照。
Graduation photo of the undergraduates in the Department of Insurance of Fudan University in 2010.

2011年复旦大学保险系本科生毕业照。
Graduation photo of the undergraduates in the Department of Insurance of Fudan University in 2011.

2012年复旦大学保险系本科生毕业照。
Graduation photo of the undergraduates in the Department of Insurance of Fudan University in 2012.

2012年复旦大学经济学院保险系十周年庆。
The 10th Anniversary of the Department of Insurance in the School of Economics of Fudan University in 2012.

2013年复旦大学保险系本科生毕业照。

Graduation photo of the undergraduates in the Department of Insurance of Fudan University in 2013.

2014年复旦大学保险系本科生毕业照。
Graduation photo of the undergraduates in the Department of Insurance of Fudan University in 2014.

2014年复旦大学保险系硕士生毕业照。
Graduation photo of the graduates in the Department of Insurance of Fudan University in 2014.

友邦-复旦精算中心二十周年庆典合影(黄云敏老师一排左一,李荣敏老师一排左二)。

The 20th Anniversary of AIA-Fudan Actuarial Centre (Huang Yunmin on the first row, first from the left; Li Rongmin on the first row, second from the left).

2015年复旦大学保险系本科生毕业照。
Graduation photo of the undergraduates in the Department of Insurance of Fudan University in 2015.

2015年复旦大学保险系硕士生毕业照。
Graduation photo of the graduates in the Department of Insurance of Fudan University in 2015.

2016年复旦大学风险管理与保险学系本科生毕业照。
Graduation photo of the undergraduates in the Department of Risk Management and Insurance of Fudan University in 2016.

2016年复旦大学风险管理与保险学系硕士生毕业照。
Graduation photo of the graduates in the Department of Risk Management and Insurance of Fudan University in 2016.

2017年复旦大学风险管理与保险学系本科生毕业照。

Graduation photo of the undergraduates in the Department of Risk Management and Insurance of Fudan University in 2017.

2017年复旦大学中国保险科技实验室团队参观上海保险交易所。

The China InsurTech Laboratory Team of Fudan University visited Shanghai Insurance Exchange in 2017.

2018年复旦大学保险科技实验室团队参观中国太平保险集团有限责任公司。
The China InsurTech Laboratory Team of Fudan University visited China Taiping Insurance Holdings in 2018.

复旦大学保险校友庆祝保险业改革开放40周年。
Insurance alumni of Fudan University celebrated the 40th anniversary of the reform and opening up of insurance industry in China.

2018年复旦大学风险管理与保险学系本科生毕业照。
Graduation photo of the undergraduates in the Department of Risk Management and Insurance of Fudan University in 2018.

2018年复旦大学风险管理与保险学系硕士生毕业照。
Graduation photo of the graduates in the Department of Risk Management and Insurance of Fudan University in 2018.

2019年复旦大学风险管理与保险学系本科生毕业照。
Graduation photo of the undergraduates in the Department of Risk Management and Insurance of Fudan University in 2019.

2019年复旦大学风险管理与保险学系硕士生毕业照。
Graduation photo of the graduates in the Department of Risk Management and Insurance of Fudan University in 2019.

　　2019年，复旦大学风险管理与保险学系一行至德国乌尔姆大学参加"第五届复旦-乌尔姆金融保险研讨会"。乌尔姆大学的经济与数学专业及精算学专业在德国排名第一。自2014年开始，复旦大学和乌尔姆大学开展了保险硕士"复旦-乌尔姆联合培养"项目，为保险行业培养了一大批具有国际视野的人才。

　　In 2019, faculties of the Department of Risk Management and Insurance from Fudan University visited Ulm University in Germany and participated in the "5th Fudan-Ulm Symposium on Finance and Insurance". Ulm University's Econo-Mathematics Program and Actuarial Program both rank first in Germany. Since 2014, Fudan University and Ulm University have carried out the Fudan-Ulm Joint Training Project for students earning a master's degree in insurance. This project has cultivated a large number of talents with an international perspective for the insurance industry.

2018 年入学的保险硕士合影。
Photo of the graduates in the Department of Risk Management and Insurance admitted in 2018.

2019 年入学的保险硕士合影。
Photo of the graduates in the Department of Risk Management and Insurance admitted in 2019.

现任复旦大学经济学院风险管理与保险学系教师（从左到右依次为：楼平易、黄煜、陈冬梅、丁纯、许闲、钱勇、段白鸽、沈婷、林琳、张仕英）。

Current faculties in the Department of Risk Management and Insurance in the School of Economics of Fudan University (from left to right: Lou Pingyi, Huang Yu, Chen Dongmei, Ding Chun, Xu Xian, Qian Yong, Duan Baige, Shen Ting, Lin Lin, and Zhang Shiying).

除了保险本科和硕士研究生教育外,复旦大学也为保险行业培养了大量优秀的博士(后)人才。

Apart from undergraduate and master's degree education programs, Fudan University has also provided a great number of PhDs and post-doctors for the insurance industry.

复旦大学校友张兴博士毕业论文,研究内容为国际保险经纪制度(2002年完成)。
The PhD thesis from Fudan University alumnus Zhang Xing, which covers the international insurance broking system (finished in 2002).

5 / 复旦保险科研回顾

复旦大学师生积极参与学术研究,其成果发表在国内外顶尖期刊上,包括《中国社会科学》《金融研究》《会计研究》, The Geneva Papers on Risk and Insurance, Insurance: Mathematics and Economics (IME), Journal of Banks and Finance (JBF)等。

Review of Insurance Research at Fudan University

Faculties and students at Fudan University have been actively engaged in academic researches, with a lot of papers published on top-tier journals, including *Social Sciences in China, Journal of Financial Research, Accounting Research, The Geneva Papers on Risk and Insurance, Insurance: Mathematics and Economics* (*IME*), *Journal of Banks and Finance* (*JBF*), etc.

医疗需求与中国医疗费用增长
——基于城乡老年医疗支出差异的视角

封 进 余央央 楼平易

摘 要：在人口老龄化和老年医疗支出城乡差异凸显的背景下，中国医疗费用增长大部分源于合理的健康需求。利用中国营养与健康调查1991—2011年的八轮数据，构造出生组跟踪样本，分别考察城乡居民医疗支出的年龄效应，估算城乡老年医疗需求导致的费用上涨，可以发现：城市居民的人均医疗支出随年龄显著增加，但农村居民的人均医疗支出随年龄增长的趋势并不明显。而忽略出生组效应，会低估城乡老年医疗支出的差距。城乡老年医疗支出差距缩小，将导致医疗费用在2010—2030年年均实际增长约5.2%。在控制医疗总费用上涨的同时，医疗保险制度需根据老年医疗需求，调整医疗资源配置结构。

关键词：医疗费用 老龄化 城乡差异

作者封进，复旦大学经济学院教授（上海 200433）；余央央，上海财经大学公共经济与管理学院讲师（上海 200433）；楼平易，新加坡南洋理工大学金融系博士生。

一、引 言

我国卫生总费用增长迅速，1990—2010年间，年均增长19%，扣除物价上涨因素，实际增长13%。[①] 近年来，控制医疗费用增长成为我国医疗卫生体制改革的目标之一。《卫生事业发展"十二五"规划》指出，必须加强对医疗费用的监管，控制医疗费用的不合理增长。现有研究大多集中于讨论一些不合理因素带来的医疗费用增长。例如，医药生产流通体制和医疗管理体制的弊端，导致药价虚高；[①] 政府投入不足，医院和医生缺乏控制医疗费用的激励等。[②] 对于由人口老龄化和城乡差距缩小等客观医疗需求带来的费用增长，现有文献研究不足。

如何甄别合理与不合理的医疗费用在实证上是一个难题。有文献认为，不合理的医疗费用是指由诱导需求引起的、相对于健康状况和病情过度提供的服务，或者是超出当前经济能力的医疗服务。[③] 但对于究竟如何判断医疗服务是否过度，文献存在很大争议。[④] 由于快速的人口老龄化和城乡医疗支出的巨大差异，相对于发达国家，我国未来的健康需求将会更大幅度地提升，因此，需要研究由此产生的医疗费用增长。考察城乡医疗费用中的年龄效应及其差异，是对医疗消费合理增长的一个较为保守的测度。这一测度有助于完善政府卫生投入机制，确定政府投入的增长幅度和医疗保险基金增长的预算，也有助于医疗保险基金对费用结构进行监控。

根据联合国人口司的预测，2030年，我国65岁以上人口数量将翻一番，达到2.35亿，65岁及以上老年人口比重将由2010年的8.4%增加到2030年的16.2%。理论上，老年人口占比增加会带来更多的健康需求，从而增加医疗消费。对OECD国家和地区医疗费用的统计发现，20世纪90年代中期，65岁及以上老人的人均医疗费用是65岁以下人口的2.7—4.8倍。[⑤] 但老龄化对医疗费用的影响在实证中仍有不同的结论，研究方法尚不够完善。尽管我国决策层和公众对老龄化下医疗费用的增长多有担忧，但对于老龄化的影响到底有多大，并无可靠的数据支撑。

城乡差异是我国的另一特征，多年来农村人均医疗支出约为城镇居民的三分之一。这一差距并非因农村居民健康状况好于城市所致。事实上，后文的数据表明，二者健康差异在各个年龄段上都不大。城乡医疗支出差异主要源于我国城乡在医疗服务供给、医疗保险覆盖和收入水平等方面的不平衡发展。今后，城乡老年医疗支出差距缩小将对医疗费用上涨产生压力。

我们采用中国营养与健康调查（CHNS）1991—2011年的八轮数据，构造出生组跟踪样本，分别考察城乡居民医疗费用中的年龄效应，通过比较城乡医疗支出随年龄增长的差异，估计出因老龄化和城乡差异缩小这一合理的健康需求产生的医疗费用增长。我们发现，城市居民人均医疗支出随年龄增长的趋势明显，但农村居民

封进、楼平易发表于《中国社会科学》的论文。
Paper by Professor Feng Jin and Lou Pingyi published in *China Social Science*.

许闲发表于《金融研究》的论文

Paper by Xu Xian published in *Journal of Financial Research*

段白鸽发表于《数量经济技术经济研究》的论文。

Paper by Duan Baige published in *The Journal of Quantitative and Technical Economics.*

许闲发表于《会计研究》的论文。
Paper by Xu Xian published in *Accounting Research*.

许闲发表于《数量经济技术经济研究》的论文。
Paper by Xu Xian published in *The Journal of Quantitative and Technical Economics*.

许闲发表于《保险研究》的论文。
Paper by Xu Xian published in *Insurance Studies*.

许闲发表于 *Environmental Hazard* 的论文。
Paper by Xu Xian published in *Environmental Hazard*.

许闲发表于 *The Geneva Papers on Risk and Insurance* 的论文。

Paper by Xu Xian published in *The Geneva Papers on Risk and Insurance*.

段白鸽发表于 *Insurance: Mathematics and Economics* 的论文。

Paper by Duan Baige published in *Insurance: Mathematics and Economics*.

许闲发表于 *Scandinavian Actuarial Journal* 的论文。

Paper by Xu Xian published in *Scandinavian Actuarial Journal*.

许闲发表于 *Transportation Research Part A: Policy and Practice* 的论文。

Paper by Xu Xian published in *Transportation Research Part A: Policy and Practice*.

许闲发表于 *Disaster Prevention and Management: An International Journal* 的论文。

Paper by Xu Xian published in *Disaster Prevention and Management: An International Journal*.

许闲发表于 *The Geneva Papers on Risk and Insurance–Issues and Practice* 的论文。

Paper by Xu Xian published in *The Geneva Papers on Risk and Insurance-Issues and Practice*.

许闲发表于 *International Journal of Climate Change Strategies and Management* 的论文。

Paper by Xu Xian published in *International Journal of Climate Change Strategies and Management.*

许闲发表于 *Journal of Banking and Finance* 的论文。

Paper by Xu Xian published in *Journal of Banking and Finance.*

楼平易发表于 Journal of Banking and Finance 的论文。

Paper by Lou Pingyi published in *Journal of Banking and Finance*.

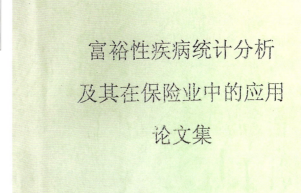

《富裕性疾病统计分析及其在保险业中的应用论文集》收录了多篇带有实地调查数据的论文，其中部分论文发表在优秀期刊上。

Collection of Papers on Statistical Analysis of Affluenza and its Application in Insurance Industry contains multiple papers with field work data, many of which are published in top-tier journals.

复旦大学保险师生积极参与国家与上海市重点课题研究,获得了一系列荣誉证书,颁奖机构包括并不限于教育部、国家减灾委员会办公室、银保监会、上海市邓小平理论研究基金理事会等。

Faculties and students in the Department of Insurance of Fudan University have been actively engaged in key research projects at both the national and Shanghai municipal levels, and have won a series of honorary recognitions. The awarding institutes include but are not limited to the Ministry of Education, Office of China National Commission for Disaster Reduction, China Banking and Insurance Regulatory Commission, the Council of Shanghai Deng Xiaoping Theory Research Fund, etc.

复旦大学保险学科所获得的部分证书。

Photos of some awards to Fudan Insurance.

徐文虎被国务院学位委员会、教育部、人力资源和社会保障部聘请为全国保险专业学位研究生教育指导委员会委员。

Xu Wenhu was appointed by the Academic Degrees Committee of the State Council, the Ministry of Education, and the Ministry of Human Resources and Social Security as a member of the Steering Committee of National Insurance Professional Degree Graduate Education.

复旦大学丁纯教授的课程"中国社会保障体系及其改革"被上海市教育委员会列为上海高校外国留学生英语授课示范性课程。

The course *China's Social Security System and Its Reform* by Professor Ding Chun at Fudan University was listed by the Shanghai Municipal Education Commission as a model of English-teaching courses for foreign students among universities in Shanghai.

许闲撰写的《灾害救助对经济增长的影响：来自中国的证据》在上海市第十二届哲学社会科学优秀成果奖（2012—2013）评选中，获论文类二等奖。

Impact of Disaster Relief on Economic Growth: Evidence from China by Xu Xian won the second prize in the thesis competition of the 12th Shanghai Philosophy and Social Sciences Outstanding Achievement Award (2012–2013).

尚汉冀、谭永基、曹沅、秦铁虎和华宣积被国家教育委员会授予国家级教学成果奖,其教学成果为"培养理论联系实际的应用数学人才",开辟精算学研究方向及培养精算人才是此项成果的内容之一。

Shang Hanji, Tan Yongji, Cao Yuan, Qin Tiehu and Hua Xuanji were given the National Teaching Achievement Award by the State Education Commission because they have "cultivated applied mathematics talents who can apply theories to practices". One of their teaching achievements was restarting actuarial research and cultivating actuarial talents.

Contribution to the Society and the Insurance Industry

Since its establishment of insurance education 100 years ago, Fudan University has nourished a huge number of insurance professionals for the society. The following precious materials witnessed the contribution Fudan insurance education has made to the difficult start of China's insurance industry.

6 / 服务社会与行业

自复旦大学百年前创办保险教育起,便为社会输送了一大批保险专业人才,以下珍贵史料无不印证了复旦保险为民族保险业艰难起步而做出的贡献。

1935年，上海市保险业同业公会第二次改选大会举行，多名复旦大学校友位列其中。

In 1935, the second re-election meeting of Shanghai Insurance Industry Association was held with the participation of a number of Fudan University alumni.

太平保险股份有限公司保险单

日期：1937年1月25日

险种为二十年两全保险。总经理周作民、协理王伯衡签名并签章。

太平保险股份有限公司1929年11月20日创立于上海，资本总额100万元，实收50万元。初名太平水火保险公司，周作民任董事长兼总经理，复旦大学校友丁雪农任协理兼上海分公司经理，经营水火保险业务。

Insurance Policy of Taiping Life Insurance Co., Ltd.

Date: January 25, 1937

The insurance policy was 20-year endowment insurance, signed and stamped by General Manager Zhou Zuomin and Associate Wang Boheng.

Taiping Life Insurance Co., Ltd. was founded in Shanghai on November 20, 1929, with a total capital of 1 million yuan and a real income of 500,000 yuan. Its former name was Taiping Marine and Fire Insurance Company, with Zhou Zuomin as the chairman and the general manager and Fudan University alumnus Ding Xuenong as the associate and the manager of its Shanghai Branch. The main business scope was fire and marine insurance.

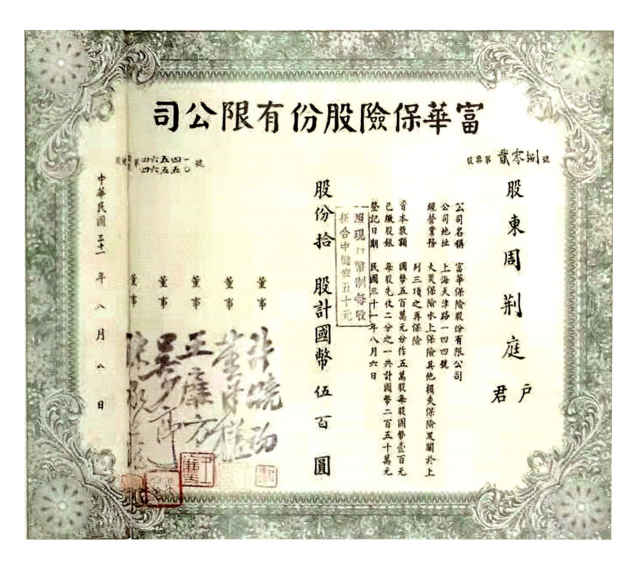

富华保险股份有限公司股票

日期：1942年8月8日

股东周荆庭，股额10股计500元（国币）。

富华保险股份有限公司1942年8月6日在上海成立，资本金500万元（中储券），实收250万元（中储券）。复旦校友许晓初任董事长兼总经理。主要经营火灾保险、水上保险、其他损失保险及关于上列三项之再保险。

Stock of Fuhua Insurance Co., Ltd.

Date: August 8, 1942

The shareholder was Zhou Jingting who owned 10 shares worth 500 yuan (currency of the Republic of China) in total.

Fuhua Insurance Co., Ltd. was established in Shanghai on August 6, 1942, with a total capital of 5 million yuan (Central Reserve Bank voucher) and a paid-up of 2.5 million yuan (Central Reserve Bank voucher). Fudan University alumnus Xu Xiaochu was the chairman and the general manager. The main business scope was fire insurance, marine insurance, other loss insurance and reinsurance on the above three items.

改革开放以来，复旦大学保险教育牢记科教兴国、人才强国的使命，主动适应社会和行业需求，通过积极举办行业论坛、开展校企合作项目、发布行业研究报告等方式为中国保险业发展和贡献智库力量，并培养出大批注重实践、勇于创新的高素质保险专业人才。

Since China's reform and opening-up, Fudan University has kept in mind its mission of rejuvenating the nation through science and education and of strengthening the nation with talents, actively adapted to the demands of the society and the insurance industry and served as a think tank for the development of China's insurance industry through organizing industry forums, conducting university-enterprise cooperation projects, and publishing industry research reports. Fudan University has cultivated a huge number of high-quality insurance professionals with practical techniques and innovative mindsets.

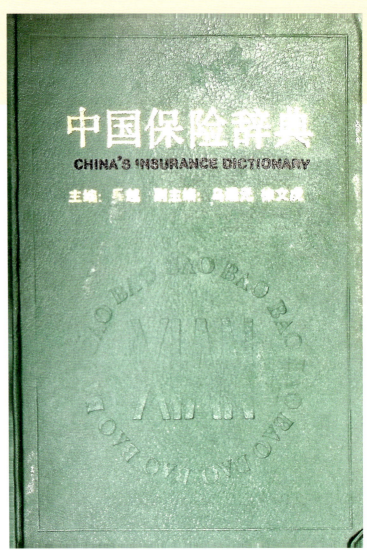

《中国保险辞典》(1989年出版)，徐文虎教授为副主编，并承担全书的编写和复审工作。该书为保险从业者重要参考书籍。

China's Insurance Dictionary (published in 1989), with Xu Wenhu as deputy chief editor, who was responsible for the compilation and review of the whole book. The book served as an important reference book for insurance practitioners.

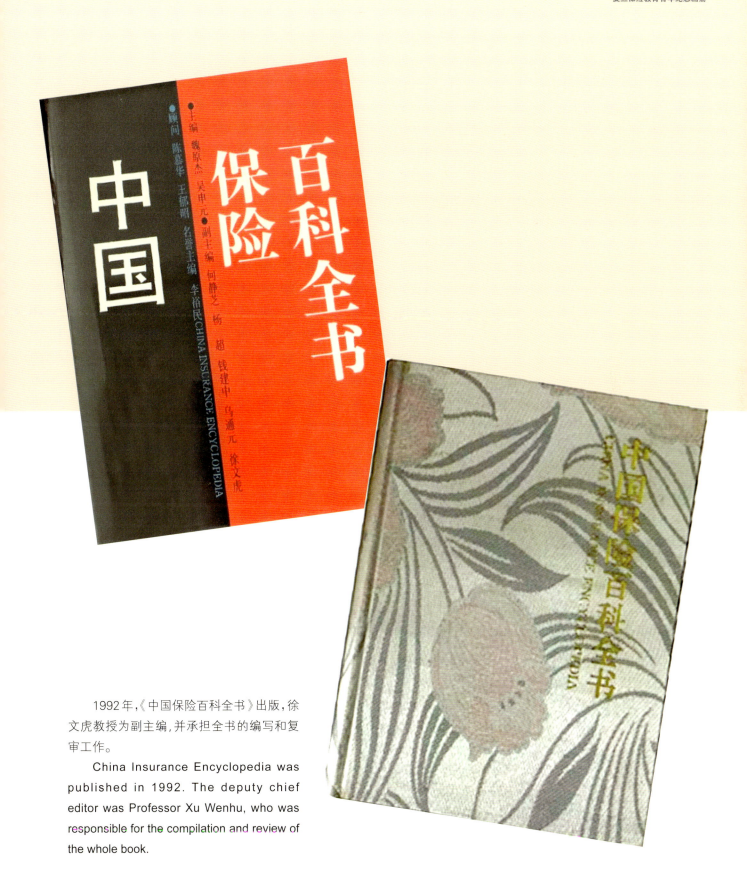

1992年,《中国保险百科全书》出版,徐文虎教授为副主编,并承担全书的编写和复审工作。

China Insurance Encyclopedia was published in 1992. The deputy chief editor was Professor Xu Wenhu, who was responsible for the compilation and review of the whole book.

2000年，时任上海市保监局局长周延礼先生（后为原保监会副主席）为复旦师生讲解保险知识。最右为汪熙教授。

In 2000, Mr. Zhou Yanli, then director-general of the Shanghai Bureau of the former China Insurance Regulatory Commission (later vice chairman of the former China Insurance Regulatory Commission), talked about the insurance market in Shanghai with faculties and students from Fudan University. On the rightmost was Professor Wang Xi.

2000年，复旦保险研究所在上海保监局支持下研究上海市保险代理人情况。

In 2000, Fudan Insurance Research Institute studied the situation of insurance agents in Shanghai with the support of the former China Insurance Regulatory Commission Shanghai Bureau.

我国加入WTO后,复旦大学连续主办三届保险博览会,为我国保险业的对外开放以及进一步发展提供支持,该博览会由复旦大学保险研究所以及上海市保险发展规划项目研究室共同承办,由复旦大学徐文虎教授担任秘书长和论坛主持人。

After China's accession to the WTO, Fudan University has hosted three Insurance Expo's with the help of the Shanghai Insurance Development Planning Project Research Office and Fudan Insurance Research Institute, providing support for the opening up and further development of China's insurance industry. Professor Xu Wenhu from Fudan University served as secretary-general and host of the forum.

2000年,复旦大学主办保险论坛商讨入世后我国保险业发展。

In 2000, Fudan University held an insurance forum to discuss the development of China's insurance industry after joining WTO.

2001年,复旦大学保险学科参与主办中国保险研讨会,话题为"入世后中国保险市场"。

In 2001, Fudan insurance co-hosted the China insurance symposium to discuss "China Insurance Market After Joining WTO".

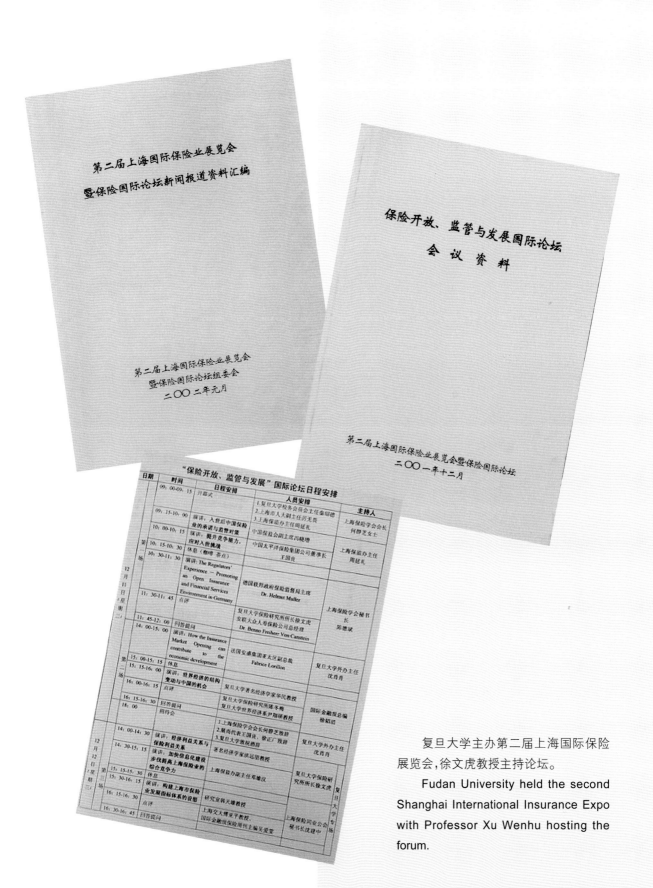

复旦大学主办第二届上海国际保险展览会,徐文虎教授主持论坛。

Fudan University held the second Shanghai International Insurance Expo with Professor Xu Wenhu hosting the forum.

三届保险博览会资料。
Handbooks of the three Insurance Expositions.

1994—1996年，为配合改革开放，加深外国对中国的了解，中央决定编纂《当代中国》系列丛书。复旦大学徐文虎教授接受《当代中国保险》的编写任务并组织编写，并最终审稿完成。该书为我国进一步开放保险业奠定了理论基石。

During 1994-1996, to accord with the reform and opening-up policy and to further foreigners' understanding of China, the Chinese central government organized the compilation of the China Contemporary series. Professor Xu Wenhu from Fudan University undertook the task of the compilation of *Contemporary Chinese Insurance*, organized the team and examined and approved the final manuscripts, laying a theoretical foundation for further opening up the insurance industry in China.

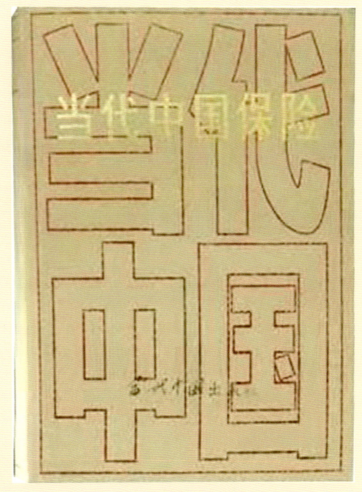

《当代中国保险》封面。
The Cover of *Contemporary Chinese Insurance*.

书中原国家领导人江泽民、李鹏、陈慕华题词。

Inscriptions in the book from former state leaders: Jiang Zeming, Li Peng, and Chen Muhua.

复旦大学积极参与上海市社保研究,取得市政府高度肯定。
Fudan University's active participation in Shanghai social insurance research was highly praised by the Shanghai municipal government.

按照当时中央指示，复旦大学徐文虎教授编写并复审《保险知识读本》，向社会普及保险知识。

According to the instructions of the Chinese central government, Professor Xu Wenhu from Fudan University participated in the compilation of *Insurance Knowledge Handbook* to disseminate insurance knowledge to the public.

复旦大学保险师生与上海新华医院共同探讨保险业如何服务医疗行业。

Faculty members and students from the Department of Insurance of Fudan University discussed with doctors from Shanghai Xinhua Hospital on how the insurance industry should serve the medical industry.

2004年,瑞士再保险公司首席经济学家何思图来沪讲学。
In 2004, Thomas Hess, chief economist of Swiss Re-insurance Company, gave lectures in Shanghai.

2005年，复旦大学主办海峡两岸保险高级论坛。
Fudan University hosted the Cross-straits Insurance Forum in 2005.

2009年，复旦大学保险研究所与上海市金融服务办公室及原中国保监会上海监管局共同完成《上海保险（再保险）交易所研究计划书》《上海保险交易所建设可行性研究》《构建中国保险交易所的可行性研究报告》，极大地推动了上海保险交易所的建立进程。2015年11月26日，国务院批准同意设立上海保险交易所。2016年6月12日，上海保险交易所正式揭牌。

In 2009, the Insurance Institute of Fudan University, in conjunction with the Shanghai Financial Services Office and the Shanghai Bureau of the former China Insurance Regulatory Commission, jointly issued *Research Plan for the Shanghai Insurance (Reinsurance) Exchange*, *Feasibility Study on the Construction of the Shanghai Insurance Exchange*, and *Feasibility Study Report on the Construction of the China Insurance Exchange*, which greatly accelerated the establishment of the Shanghai Insurance Exchange. On November 26, 2015, the State Council approved the establishment of the Shanghai Insurance Exchange. On June 12, 2016, the Shanghai Insurance Exchange was officially opened.

2009年,复旦大学主办保险高级论坛暨吴家錄先生捐赠仪式。
In 2009, Fudan University hosted the Senior Forum on Insurance—Mr. Wu Jialu's Donation Ceremony.

Contribution to the Society and the Insurance Industry

2015年,复旦大学中国保险与社会安全研究中心主办上海论坛保险分论坛"巨灾风险管理与金融创新",引导社会关注巨灾风险。

In 2015, the China Insurance and Social Security Research Center of Fudan University hosted the sub-forum of the Shanghai Forum with the theme "Catastrophe Risk Management and Financial Innovation" to attract the social attention to catastrophe risks.

2016年，复旦大学中国保险与社会安全研究中心主办上海论坛保险分论坛，聚焦"一带一路中的灾害防御与救灾合作"。

The China Insurance and Social Security Research Center of Fudan University hosted the insurance sub-forum of the 2016 Shanghai Forum which focused on "Disaster Prevention and Relief Cooperation in the Belt and Road Initiative".

2017年,复旦大学主办全球金融消费者研讨会。
In 2017, Fudan University hosted the Global Forum for Financial Consumers.

2017年，复旦大学中国保险科技实验室主办上海论坛分保险论坛："保险科技：新市场、新生态、新引擎。"

The China InsurTech Laboratory of Fudan University hosted the sub-forum of the 2017 Shanghai Forum with the theme "InsurTech: New Market, New Ecology and New Engine".

2018年，复旦大学中国保险科技实验室主办上海论坛保险分论坛，复旦大学中国保险科技实验室发布《人工智能保险行业运用路线图》。时任上海保险同业公会秘书长赵雷、复旦发展研究院执行副院长张怡等发表演讲。

In 2018, The China InsurTech Laboratory of Fudan University hosted the insurance sub-forum of the Shanghai Forum. The China InsurTech Laboratory of Fudan University released *Road Map for the Application of Artificial Intelligence in Insurance Industry*. Zhao Lei, who was then the secretary-general of Shanghai Insurance Association, with Zhang Yi, vice executive dean of Fudan Development Institute (FDI) and other guests delivered speeches at the forum.

2019年，复旦保险主办上海论坛保险分论坛，关注女性健康并发布《女性健康保险白皮书》。

In 2019, the Department of Insurance and Risk Maragement of Fudan University hosted the insurance sub-forum of the Shanghai Forum to focus on female health and released *White Papers of Female Health Insurance*.

原保监会副主席魏迎宁应邀参加2019上海论坛。

Wei Yingning, vice chairman of the former China Insurance Regulatory Commission, was invited by Fudan Insurance to attend the Shanghai Forum in 2019.

复旦大学党委书记焦扬在2019年上海论坛保险分论坛致辞。

Jiao Yang, secretary of the Party Committee of Fudan University, delivered a speech at the insurance sub-forum of the Shanghai Forum in 2019.

复旦大学常务副校长桂永浩在2019年上海论坛保险分论坛演讲。

Gui Yonghao, executive vice president of Fudan University, delivered a speech at the insurance sub-forum of the Shanghai Forum in 2019.

复旦大学保险学科依托复旦发展研究院,向政府提交了一系列的内参报告(由于保密性的要求,仅可提供极有限的图片)。

Fudan Insurance, with the Fudan Development Institute, has submitted a series of internal reference reports to the government. (Due to confidentiality requirements, only very limited pictures can be provided.)

7 / 社会各界对复旦保险的寄语

100年，漫漫求索，中流击水。

100年，峥嵘岁月，风雨华章。

满百载初心不改，跨世纪薪火相传。站在新起点上的复旦保险人必将凝心聚力、砥砺前行，必将守正创新、引领未来！

Words from All Walks of Life to Fudan Insurance

Throughout the 100 years, we have explored through a long journey and striven hard to our commitment.

Throughout the 100 years, we have witnessed the glorious days and conquered all the hardships.

The ambition remains unchanged after 100 years and the torch was passed down across the century. On the threshold of a new start, everyone of Fudan Insurance will gather together to move on and keep the innovation to lead the future!

> 培养保险人才
> 服务保险事业
>
> 秦绍德
> 一九九九年十月

复旦大学原党委书记秦绍德寄语复旦保险。
Words to Fudan Insurance from Qin Shaode, former secretary of the Party Committee of Fudan University.

> 把[安盛—国卫]复旦保险研究中心建设成为
> 国内一流的保险研究基地
>
> 王生洪
> 一九九九年十月

复旦大学原校长、上海市政协原副主席王生洪寄语复旦保险。
Words to Fudan Insurance from Wang Shenghong, former president of Fudan University and former vice chairman of the Shanghai Political Consultative Conference.

复旦大学原副校长施岳群教授寄语复旦保险。

Words to Fudan Insurance from Professor Shi Yuequn, former vice president of Fudan University.

中国保险 保险中国
贺母校保险专业100年
施岳群
2019.1.12

保险万古长青
洪远朋
2019.1.12.

复旦大学经济学院原院长洪远朋教授寄语复旦保险。

Words to Fudan Insurance from Professor Hong Yuanpeng, former dean of the School of Economics, Fudan University.

复旦大学经济学院保险系原副系主任徐培华教授寄语复旦保险。

Words to Fudan Insurance from Professor Xu Peihua, former deputy director of the Department of Insurance, School of Economics, Fudan University.

百年前的曙光，照耀着复旦保险专业前程的辉煌
贺复旦保险专业百年纪念 徐培华

复旦大学校友，史带财险董事长张兴寄语复旦保险。

Words to Fudan Insurance from Fudan alumnus, Zhang Xing, the chairman of STARR Property & Casualty Insurance Company.

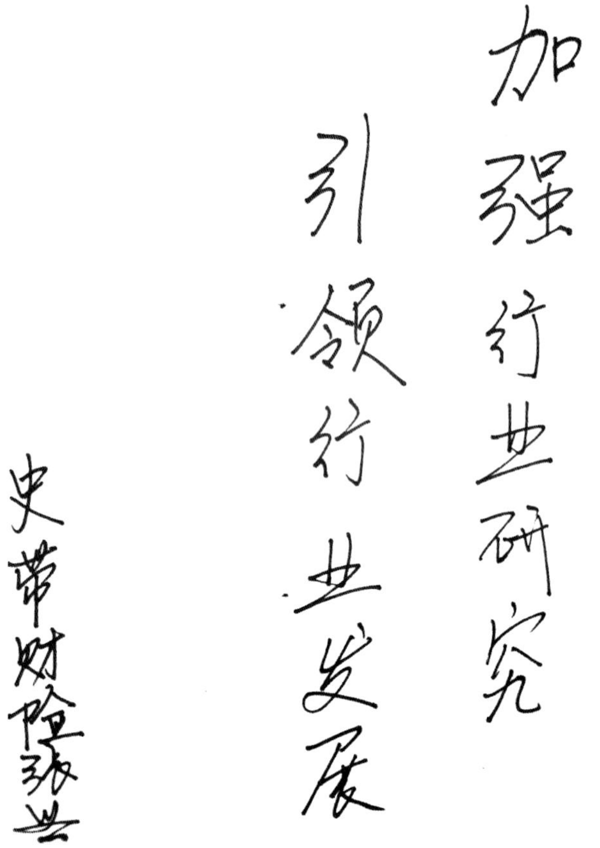

加强行业研究
引领行业发展

史带财险张兴

1984届复旦大学保险校友周伟国寄语复旦保险。

Words to Fudan Insurance from Fudan Insurance alumnus Zhou Weiguo who graduated in 1984.

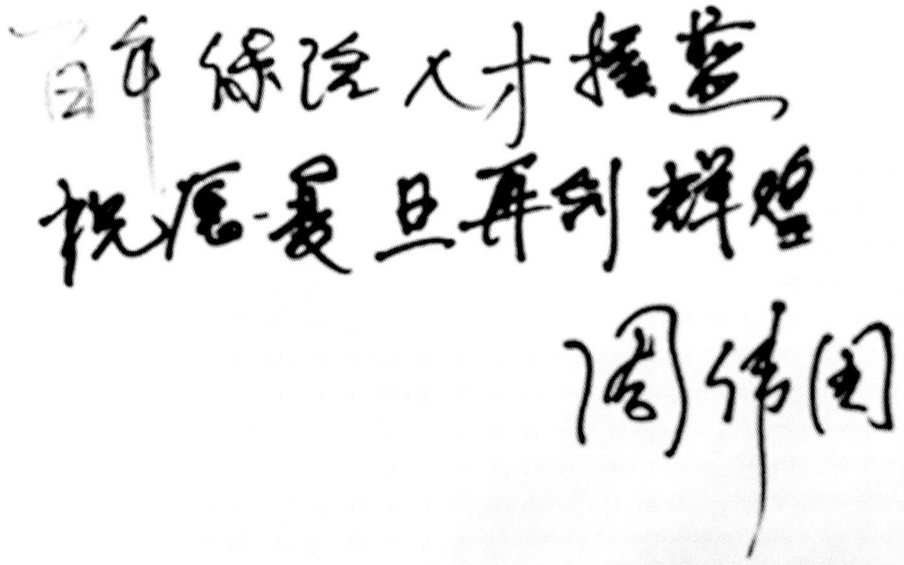

百年保险人才摇篮
祝愿复旦再创辉煌

周伟国

樊纲2013年访问复旦大学并寄语复旦保险。
Words to Fudan Insurance from Fan Gang when he visited Fudan University in 2013.

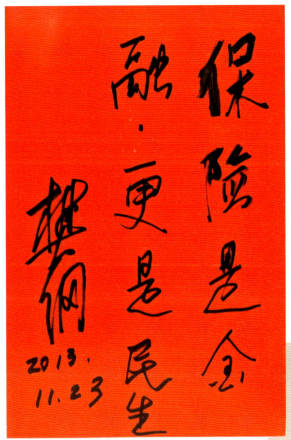

I have high expectations for the Chinese insurance industry!
Robert J. Shiller
May 23, 2014

2014年，2013年诺贝尔经济学奖得主席勒访问复旦大学，寄语中国保险。
Words to China insurance from Schiller, the 2013 laureate of Nobel prize in Economics, when he visited Fudan University in 2014.

Shanghai 25.5.2015

I would like to express my best wishes for China's Insurance Industry in the interest of a growing financial system.

Saccomanni
Former Minister of Economy and Finance of Italy

2015年，意大利前经济财政部长萨科曼尼（Fabrizio Saccomanni）访问复旦大学，寄语中国保险。

Words to China insurance from Fabrizio Saccomanni, Italy's former Minister of Economy and Finance, when he visited Fudan University in 2015.

The insurance industry is going through a huge transformation. Understanding risk and being proactive in risk management is a large growth area. Insurance is one industry that will benefit from advanced thinking in proactive risk management.

Myron Scholes
05/23/2015

2015年，1997年诺贝尔经济学奖得主迈伦·斯科尔斯访问复旦大学，寄语中国保险。

Words to China insurance from Myron Scholes, the 1997 laureate of Nobel Prize in Economics, when he visited Fudan University in 2015.

后 记

《复旦保险教育百年纪念画册》付梓在即，在编撰画册和整理史料的过程中，指梢间，复旦保险教育百年历史如长河般流过：或自小溪流而始，那是整整一百年前列强肆虐、山河破碎之时，复旦保险先辈们于商科开设保险课程；或途经戈壁，那是抗战时，复旦保险先辈们坚持保留保险选修课；或水丰草茂，那是中华人民共和国成立时复旦大学立刻恢复保险教育；或大河奔腾，那是改革开放后，复旦保险积极培养保险人才，支持行业发展，服务国家战略。同时，一股强烈的历史感、荣誉感、责任感自心底升腾而起，不可平息。

历史感来自复旦保险教育的整整百年信史。1919年，正值民族积贫积弱，巴黎和会列强欺辱中华，伴随着五四运动救亡图存的，是复旦公学（当时之公学指民间共同筹款而建之学校）秉承"读书不忘救国，救国不忘读书"，于商学院开设保险课程。次年，复旦公学修改章程，开设"保险学""保险簿记""保险利息算学""保险学原理"四门保险课程。1927年，复旦大学修改章程引入学分制，将"保险学"设为四学分必修课，并将"水险""火险""寿险"设为选修课。抗战时，复旦保险教育似星火般闪烁，商学院统计系学生可选修"保险学"。1949年中华人民共和国成立后，复旦大学立刻恢复保险教育，法学院社会学系开设"社会保险""劳动保险"，商学院开设"保险学""保险合作"等。从事复旦保险教育者，是一位位名字闪耀中国保险教育历史的先生：周德熙，复旦大学教授，江苏江宁人，美国伊利诺伊大学硕士毕业，主持复旦保险教育十余年；王效文，复旦大学兼职教授，被称为"中国保险学理论研究的拓荒者"；周绍濂，1946年起为复旦大学教授，其编撰的《人寿保险计算学》为中国第一本精算教材。

荣誉感来自复旦保险支持行业发展、服务国家使命的光荣传承。在外资保险公司林立的旧上海，民族保险业团结一致，成立上海市同业公会，其中不乏复旦大学校友的身影，如太平保险第一协理丁雪农、富华保险董事长兼总经理许晓初等。改革开放后，复旦保险更是身处中国保险业发展的前沿，承担高校社会责任。复旦保险以学报国，帮助中国人民银行培养金融干部，按照当时的中央部署，徐文虎教授参与编撰《中国保险辞典》《当代中国保险》《中国保险全书》等新中国重要保险书籍，研究上海保交所可行性及筹备方案；尚汉冀教授主持友邦－复旦精算中心工作，培养中国精算人才近500名。与此同时，复旦保险化作中外保险业的桥梁，为安盛、纽约人寿、中美大都会等国际保险巨头入华合法经营牵线搭桥，共同研究，共同办会。复旦保险为民族保险业更是输送了一批又一批人才，40年来，从开设太平洋保险班，到为中国人民保险公司培养高级保险干部，复旦保险不遗余力，发挥专长，以教研帮助民族保险业振兴。

责任感来自复旦保险紧跟保险行业发展、创新保险教育的时代要求。近年来，在不进则退的保险教育改革中，复旦保险勇于创新、不落人后。保险科技日新月异，正深刻地改变保险这一古老的行业，复旦保险积极参与保险科技学术研究，出版多本保险科技的书籍以及研究报告，多次举办保险科技论坛，为行业提供学术支持。2019年秋季开始，复旦保险为全校学生开设"保险科技"课程，广聚各专业英才；保险精算历久弥新，复旦大学于2019年9月正式成为英国精算师协会考试豁免认证高校，是中国大陆唯一一所首次递交申请即获得全部6门核心课程（core principles）考试豁免的综合性高校。以上成就来自时刻萦绕于心头的责任感，而这种来自百年保险教育历史的责任，也是复旦保险不断前行的不竭动力。

这本画册记录的复旦保险的前一百年，也是我国从积贫积弱发展到现在即将全面建成小康社会的一百年。在中国继续高质量发展的征程中，保险业将在科技的催化下继续保有活力，而复旦保险在以上的良好环境下，在我们一代又一代复旦保险人的传承下，定将迎来更为璀璨的下一个一百年！

是为后记。

2019年10月1日于复旦大学经济学院

图书在版编目(CIP)数据

复旦保险教育百年纪念画册:汉英对照/徐文虎,许闲主编. —上海:复旦大学出版社,2019.12
ISBN 978-7-309-14710-0

Ⅰ.①复… Ⅱ.①徐… ②许… Ⅲ.①复旦大学经济学院-校史-画册 Ⅳ.①G649.285.1-64

中国版本图书馆 CIP 数据核字(2019)第 241881 号

复旦保险教育百年纪念画册:汉英对照
徐文虎 许 闲 主编
责任编辑/方毅超 李 荃

复旦大学出版社有限公司出版发行
上海市国权路 579 号 邮编:200433
网址: fupnet@ fudanpress.com   http://www.fudanpress.com
门市零售: 86-21-65642857   团体订购: 86-21-65118853
外埠邮购: 86-21-65109143
上海雅昌艺术印刷有限公司印刷

开本 889×1194 1/16 印张 10 字数 150 千
2019 年 12 月第 1 版第 1 次印刷

ISBN 978-7-309-14710-0/G·2047
定价:198.00 元

如有印装质量问题,请向复旦大学出版社有限公司发行部调换。
版权所有   侵权必究